Early Settler Activity Guide

Elizabeth Stenson

The Early Settler Life Series

Crabtree Publishing Company

A special thanks to **Carla Williams** for her contribution of activities and editorial expertise.

Many thanks also to the following people without whose help this guide would not have been possible.

Editor-in-chief: Bobbie Kalman
Senior editor: Lise Gunby
Assistant editors: Susan Hughes
Marilyn Waplington
Original artwork: Meeae Kim
Design and mechanicals: Diane Taylor
Nancy Cook

Cataloging in Publication Data

Stenson, Elizabeth
Early Settler Activity Guide

(Early settler life series)
Supplement to titles in The Early settler life series.
ISBN 0-86505-036-8

1. Frontier and pioneer life – Study and teaching (Elementary).
I. Title. II. Series.

LB1581.S83 1983   372.8'9044

102 Torbrick Avenue
Toronto M4J 4Z5

350 Fifth Avenue
Suite 3308
New York, N.Y. 10001

Contents

Why study the early settlers?

The settlers were a hardy, resourceful, and ingenious people who came from the far corners of the earth to create new lives for themselves.

● Studying the everyday lives of the settlers provides an opportunity to explore a society from its inception, and to examine the need of every society for food, shelter, and culture.

● Students are exposed to the concept of communities: what communities are, how they begin and develop, how they relate to the environment, what makes them cohere. Students can compare life in communities of the past with life in communities today.

● Comparing a past way of life to the present helps students examine and understand change in the physical, social, and cultural environment, and factors that precipitate change.

● Students can learn to respect a variety of attitudes toward values and customs.

● Students begin to appreciate artifacts of the past, what can be learned from these, and the importance of preserving them.

● Learning about early settler communities sets a context for the study of the history of the students' own community.

● These social history studies provide an excellent means of developing such language skills as locating, organizing, and presenting information from a variety of sources.

● Finally, learning about the early settlers can be fascinating fun. There are plenty of opportunities for students to get involved in discussion and role playing, and to participate in creating useful and beautiful objects.

The Early Settler Activity Guide will help you to get started and be a source of ideas and information throughout your studies.

The chapters are organized topically as centers of interest rather than periods of historical significance. Each chapter contains a preface with conceptual objectives for that chapter, a brief content summary, references to the appropriate Early Settler Life books, and notes to the teacher.

Organization of the guide

The first three chapters establish the groundwork, and set the context for further studies. It is suggested that these chapters be dealt with in sequence. Selected activities from the other chapters may be interspersed wherever appropriate.

After that, you may wish to pursue the material in accordance with your own priorities and the students' interests.

THE CHAPTER HEADINGS

The chapters are as follows:

1 **Coming to a New Land** (the settlers arrive)

2 **A Homestead Grows** (early homes and farms)

3 **The Village Established** (early communities)

4 **Homespun** (homecrafts, clothing, health)

5 **Bread on the Table** (food and food preparation)

6 **A Hard Day's Work** (occupations, artisans, the sawmill)

7 **See You at the Store** (stores and markets)

8 **Reading, 'Riting, and 'Rithmetic** (learning and schools)

9 **Little Adults** (treatment of children)

10 **Making Connections** (transportation and communication)

11 **Box Socials** (pleasures and pastimes; holidays)

USING THE EARLY SETTLER LIFE SERIES

Many of the activities in this guide are based on information presented in the Early Settler Life Series. Relevant page numbers and cross-references among texts are provided. Numerous activities are designed for individual and small group work, for classes possessing partial sets of books. Also included are many activities which do not require reference to the Early Settler Life Series. Thus, the activity guide is easily accommodated to a variety of classroom and resource center situations.

The Early Settler Life Series provides a wealth of information for your students. You are encouraged, however, to supplement the series with any other resources you have available: films, filmstrips, pictures, and other reference texts.

a) Terminology

The term used through this guide and the series is "settler" rather than "pioneer." A pioneer is defined as a person who ventures into unknown or unclaimed territory to settle. While many of the settlers were indeed pioneers, many were not, in the true sense of the word. We suggest that you clarify this distinction with your students.

Other terms may cause occasional confusion during research. Some sources will differentiate between "log cabin" and "shanty," for example, while others will treat them synonymously. "Chemist," "apothecary," and "druggist" might all be used to describe the same occupation. As early settler study covers quite a long time frame and different locales, this variation in terminology is bound to occur.

b) Time Frame and Geographical Differences

The Early Settler Life Series spans a time frame from the mid-1700s to the late nineteenth century. Conditions differed both across time and across the country. Simply explain to students that conditions differed from place to place, as more and more settlers arrived, and as the country developed. The time span will help students begin to understand the types of changes that occurred and the effect these changes had on the settlers' lives.

The emphasis of the series is on the **process** of settlement; therefore, the series is applicable to different times and places. The series is about **people.** Stress the human aspect. Concentration on dates is confusing and frustrating to younger students.

WERE YOU A PIONEER, MISS WINSTON?

Getting started: Coming to grips with the past

The idea of historical time is developed slowly and only after considerable experience and learning. The above cartoon suggests a child's grasp of time span, in which a decade and a century may well seem equivalent. Early settler study can help students begin to understand past time.

Creating a simple time line is a good way to start. Begin with time lines of the students' own lives, marking special events and happenings of significance to them.

Next, establish a time line using counters or markers to represent one year. (You will need about 200 counters — beans will do nicely if you don't have counters.) Explain that each 25 counters represents about one generation, expressed as "when your parents were young," "when your grandparents were young," etcetera. Count out about 200 markers to represent the time period you will be learning about.

Have students establish whose time they will be learning about. It will likely come

out as "when our great-great-great-great-great-great-grandparents were young." Explain that your studies will be from about then until the time their great-great-grandparents were young.

Creating a classroom environment

During the time you are involved in learning about the early settlers, try to establish an interesting and appealing environment within the classroom. The activities suggested in this guide should produce a wealth of pictures and products with which to build displays. Make these three-dimensional whenever possible.

Collect resources — books, picture collections, articles, etc. — and have these on hand.

Buy or borrow as many artifacts or reproductions as you can. Those which are fragile or of great value should be displayed in a safe location.

1972	I was born.
1973	I learned to walk and talk.
1974	I fell and broke my arm.
1975	I started nursery school. My grandmother came to live with us.
1976	We moved to 36 Church St. I started school.
1977	My baby sister was born.
1978	I got a two-wheel bike.
1979	I broke my front teeth. I went to Disneyland.
1980	My mom went to work.
1981	I joined the swim team. I went to summer camp.
1982	I got a paper route.

EARLY SETTLER COSTUMES

Your activities will seem much more authentic if you can all dress the part. Try to have your students assemble costumes which can be worn on several different occasions. A letter home to parents, well ahead of time, explaining what you will be doing and offering suggestions for assembling costumes, usually pays off. Given a little time, most will be cooperative and helpful.

BOYS' COSTUMES

These can be very simple — knee socks pulled over trouser legs produce instant knickers. Top these with a white shirt, suspenders, a little black tie, and a plain cap.

GIRLS' COSTUMES

These can also be simple. While most pattern companies have patterns for "pioneer dresses" and some parents might wish to make dresses, it is not really necessary to go to this trouble. An old cotton skirt of mother's (maybe with the hem let down for the taller girls) can be topped by a simple white blouse and a long apron. Simple cotton aprons could be made in class by the students themselves. Dark stockings or knee socks may be worn underneath.

Why not make a costume for the teacher, too!

Visit an old cemetery.

Reaching out

A high quality learning experience requires that your students have things to do, see, hear, touch, and react to. Going on field trips and bringing visitors into the classroom can provide such experiences.

FIELD TRIPS

(a) Museums and restorations (homes, schools, entire villages) are ideal locations. Try to find one that offers a participation program where students may take part in such activities as open-hearth cooking, broom-making, candle-dipping, weaving, and woodworking.

(b) Consider other historical sites. Even if students are not ready to fully appreciate the historical significance of the particular site, such a visit can provide one more opportunity to glimpse some aspect of the past.

(c) If your community has an older or original section, consider a walking tour to observe the buildings and the ways they were built. Perhaps a private citizen who lives in an older home would welcome the opportunity to "show off" his/her "heirloom" to a group of interested, well-supervised students!

(d) A visit to an old cemetery can be most interesting. Try to have something you'd like to find out before going: What was the average lifespan? Are there many children's graves? Are there any famous people buried there? How did the life spans of men and women compare? Did many babies die at birth?

(e) If you promise to be very careful, a local antique dealer may let you visit his/her place of business. Such a visit would be best done in small groups, perhaps with the help of volunteer parents.

VISITORS

(a) Is there a curator or staff person from a local museum or university who would be willing to visit your class and perhaps bring along a few artifacts? Make sure you inform your visitor beforehand about what you have been studying and what you hope the students will learn from the visit.

(b) Local amateur historians, usually members of local historical societies, often appreciate the opportunity to share what they have learned or to talk about their latest project. These people can be especially valuable when you wish to focus on your local community history.

(c) Many craftspeople are involved in practicing crafts that were part of the daily lives of the early settlers — spinning, weaving, dyeing, candlemaking. Many are delighted to demonstrate their craft. Local craft societies or organizations may be able to direct you to the appropriate people.

(d) Do you have a local "little theater" group who may have costumes to show, or plays to present to your class?

(e) Is there a parent, grandparent, or relative who has knowledge of some aspect of early settler life or owns some interesting antiques, who would be willing to come and talk with your class? Assure those who've never done this sort of thing before that they don't have to teach a lesson — your students will have all the questions. (Questions submitted beforehand are usually appreciated.)

MAKING THE MOST OF THE EXPERIENCE

Be well prepared beforehand and record as much as possible during the trip or visit so that you have something tangible to help you recall what you saw and heard.

Take along a tape recorder — record any interviews, music, or interesting sounds. Include a time for sketching and take along materials so that impressions may be captured on the spot.

Taking photographs (try using student photographers) is a worthwhile method of recording your outing or visit. Photographs can later be displayed, or used to illustrate a booklet about the event. You might want a few costumed students to act out situations which could be photographed.

The following activities are ones which can be used as a culmination to your early settler studies or which can be sustained throughout your studies.

AN ANCESTOR GALLERY

Nearly everyone has an old family album. Encourage students to bring old photos to school. Hang these on a bulletin board to create an ancestor gallery. Have students paint "portraits" of great-great-grandfather or grandmother as they might have looked. Try to portray any family traits.

SHADY LANE SCHOOL MUSEUM

Why not create your own early settler museum? You might house it in an empty classroom or space in your school. If not, reserve a corner of the classroom for this purpose. Include items which students have brought to school, art activities, models, and pictures. Create description cards for various items and displays. You might even catalog your collection. When your museum is complete, invite the public (other classes, parents, school guests) to tour. Send out hand-lettered invitations describing your collection and noting viewing hours.

Create an early settler "picture dictionary." Begin by collecting as many early settler words as possible for each letter of the alphabet. Have each student responsible for one or two pages. Assemble the completed pages to form a book.

A MODEL EXPERIENCE

Create a model of an early village, complete with landscape, buildings, gardens, wagons, people, and animals. A sandbox makes an ideal setting; alternatively, use a table top, creating the physical background by using salt/flour relief. A more ambitious undertaking is to create a walk-through village if space permits. Each student creates a building using cardboard cartons. These are arranged on the floor down a "main street" (large pieces of brown paper stuck to the floor).

Create a model of a settler home. If space permits, build a walk-through village.

THE SEASONS PASS

Keep a seasonal "calendar" of early settler activities. Begin with four large charts, one each for summer, fall, winter, and spring. As you progress through your studies, record any seasonal activities on the appropriate chart.

Saying goodbye to relatives was a heartbreaking experience. Many of these people never saw each other again. A new life meant giving up many of the people you loved.

Chapter 1: Coming to a new land

Objectives

A context for further studies of the early settlers.

The hardships and challenges faced by the early settlers.

The impact of the environment on the early settler way of life.

The concept of self-sufficiency as it applied to the early settler way of life.

Respect for their perseverence and industry.

Early Settler Series references

Early Village Life
The Early Family Home
Early Travel
Early Loggers and the Sawmill
Early Farm Life
Early Settler Storybook
Early Stores and Markets

Contents

- who the early settlers were

- why they journeyed to a new land

- how they traveled

- establishment of first farms

- how basic needs of food and shelter were met

- how the land was cleared

- the hard lot and strenuous work of the first settlers

- the role of the environment in determining a way of life

- hazards and problems faced by the settlers

Notes to the teacher

The concept of settlement may be approached from the children's experiences of moving to a new home, school, or town.

Children may be prepared for the concept of emigration to a new land by reviewing their knowledge of migration of birds and of changes of habitat among animals for various reasons and purposes: seasonal appropriateness, natural disasters, survival needs.

Unlike migrations in the animal kingdom, human families have much to consider when moving to a new location.

The following activity may be duplicated for individual research at home. Children with large families may wish to interview a number of members.

Children with a long history of stable family locale can be encouraged to participate imaginatively and to research travel poems and stories to share with the class.

Children without parents or family will find their experiences dealt with sympathetically in the Early Settler Series.

Using the research

The results of this study will suggest many creative possibilities suitable for your class. The following are some suggestions:

● Construct a chart on feelings and emotions for later comparison with the early settlers' experiences.

● Children may start a class picture collection, to locate scenes that clearly show facial expressions and/or expressive body postures. Have them mount their finds on individual cards of matching size, and store them in a box for later use.

● Construct bar graphs on travel methods: air, land, and ship.

A covering note should accompany the interview sheets, stating the purpose of this study.

ON OUR WAY

Making the decision

Who decided to make the move?
How did you feel about it?
What did you know about the new home?
How did you find out?
What did you decide to take with you?
What did you leave behind?

The Journey

When did you make the trip?
How did you travel?
Did you stop along the way to visit other places?
How long did the trip take?
Who came with you?
What was the trip like?

The Arrival

What were your first impressions of the new location?
Did anyone greet you?
Did you feel like a stranger?
What did you miss from your former place?
What were the advantages and disadvantages of the new location?

ARRIVAL ACTIVITIES

Examine relevant maps and point out the global journeys.

Incorporate arithmetic problems incidentally using distance figures.

Discuss ways and means of greeting newcomers to the school and the neighborhood, and making them feel welcome.

If children have old family photo albums, encourage them to ask permission to bring these to school to share with the class.

Construct a display called **Hands Around the World:**

Draw an outline of a map of the world or use a wall map. Have children make a cutout of a hand, print own name on it, and a sentence such as, "My family came here ____ years ago from _____ (eg. Puerto Rico)." Arrange the hands all around the map and attach each to the place of origin with yarn.

MY ROOTS

Construct a poster called **My Roots in the Past.** This will be a family tree, showing generations and relationships from the "family pioneer" to the present.

MY FAMILY TREE

A THOUSAND QUESTIONS

Many early settlers had limited knowledge of what awaited them in the new land. Have groups of students compose a list of questions they think would have been going through the minds of the settlers as they first sighted their new land. Share the lists. Keep a record of the questions to use at the end of Chapter 1.

To review and consolidate the unit, discuss answers to the questions listed at the beginning of this activity or present a question and answer sheet as a "matching exercise."

Alternately, pupils may illustrate the contrast between aspects of "the dream" and "the reality."

The reality of the New World.

NOBODY FOR MILES

Creative writing topic:

You are going to be camping for two weeks in a remote area. You can take with you only what you can carry, and can choose one person to accompany you. You will have to be largely self-sufficient.

What are the most important items to take?

What must you consider when choosing what to take?

What kind of person would it be best to choose to have along?

What do you need to learn before you leave?

Write the plan for your trip.

Crowd aboard!

1. <u>Who came to the new land?</u>

- explorers
- fur traders
- farmers
- business people
- soldiers
- people from many countries including England, Scotland, Ireland, Germany and France

2. <u>Why did they come?</u>

- to seek a better life
- to get land of their own
- to start farms and businesses
- to find jobs
- to be free
- to get away from war
- to get away from famine
- to find adventure
- it was too crowded in Europe

3. <u>How did they get here?</u>

- by ship, often in the hold
- the trip often took as long as two months
- there was little food and water
- many became seasick and ill, and many died of disease

A BETTER LIFE

Prepare a large chart using the headings below. Have groups of students research the questions using **Early Travel,** pp. 8–11, **Early Stores and Markets,** p. 4, and any other available sources.

Your finished chart might resemble the one in the next column. Discuss your findings.

SAMANTHA'S STORY

Read Samantha Stell's account of her first experiences as a settler, **The Early Family Home,** pp. 7–9.

Discuss:

What were the first things the settlers had to consider upon reaching their land?

Focus on the necessity to meet such basic needs as food, water, shelter, clearing the land.

Have groups of students dramatize the arrival of the Stell family at their land.

BARE NECESSITIES

Once the family arrived, they still had a long and arduous journey over rough roads and trails to their land. These journeys were made on foot or by cart. Supplies were limited by the family's ability to carry them and to afford them. Most settlers had brought few goods with them in their "hand baggage."

Distribute the following list of items and have students research those with which they are unfamiliar.

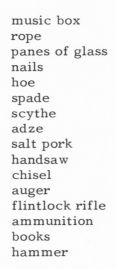

dishes	music box
cutlery	rope
pail	panes of glass
kettle	nails
pots	hoe
table	spade
rocking chair	scythe
crib	adze
mattresses	salt pork
candles	handsaw
ax	chisel
knife	auger
fishing gear	flintlock rifle
seed	ammunition
flour	books
blankets/bedding	hammer

Discuss the items. Decide which would be necessities and which could be done without.

Make a list of the items in terms of their priority, researching their authentic appearances if possible, and form a composite picture with this material.

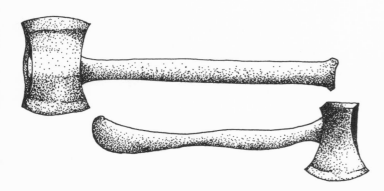

Have students research methods and implements used to clear land. **Early Loggers and the Sawmill**, pp. 4-7, is a good place to start.

Write an instruction sheet or manual on "How to Clear Land."

Discuss:

Why was it so important to clear the land?

What made it such backbreaking work?

Why was it absolutely necessary to begin preparing for winter right away? What preparations were made?

What could the settlers eat while waiting for their first crops to mature?

BASIC NEEDS

Among the first tasks of the settlers were the building of some sort of shelter (usually a shanty or even a lean-to), starting to clear the land, and preparing for winter.

Examine the text in **The Early Family Home**, p. 4, **Early Village Life**, pp. 4-5, and **Early Loggers and the Sawmill**, pp. 4-9.

Various types of shanty, lean-to, and early home details are given in **The Early Family Home**, p. 9, and **Early Loggers and the Sawmill**, pp. 4-12.

WORK, WORK, WORK

Here is Samantha Stell's poem, "Work," from **The Early Family Home,** p. 9.

> Work! for the night is coming;
> Work! through the morning hours;
> Work! while the dew is sparkling;
> Work! 'mid the springing flowers;
> Work! while the day grows brighter,
> Under the flowing sun;
> Work! for the night is coming,
> Night — when our work is done.
> Work! for the night is coming;
> Work! through the sunny noon,
> Fill the bright hours with labor;
> Rest cometh sure and soon.
> Give to each flying minute
> Something to keep in store;
> Work! for the night is coming;
> Night — when we work no more.

Discuss:

What would it be like to have to work so hard?

What would happen if the settlers failed to work hard?

Have students compose their own early settler work poems. The following model will help avoid stilted and contrived rhyming:

> Work to clear the land
> Work to build a shanty
> Work to stay alive
> Work from dawn to dusk
> Tiring, endless, backbreaking work!

Try writing poems to other models.

A HOUSEWARMING SYMBOL

Marcus Stell writes a poem to hang on the wall. On p. 11 of **The Early Family Home,** this poem is called an "official housewarming symbol." Discuss the meaning of this term. Are the students familiar with any housewarming customs today? (The most basic is to take a gift to friends when you visit their new home for the first time.)

A SELF-SUFFICIENCY INDEX

The Stell family is self-sufficient in another way. They are educated. They can read, write, and entertain each other. They gain a great deal of satisfaction from relying on themselves. They can see what they need to do, and they know, or can find out, how to do it.

Have students create a self-sufficiency index of their own skills, using the following headings:

What I can do for myself
How I need others to help me
What I want to learn to do for myself
Who can teach me these things
When do I expect to learn them

(Refer to the activity, SKILLS EXCHANGE, Chapter 7)

A WORK OF ART

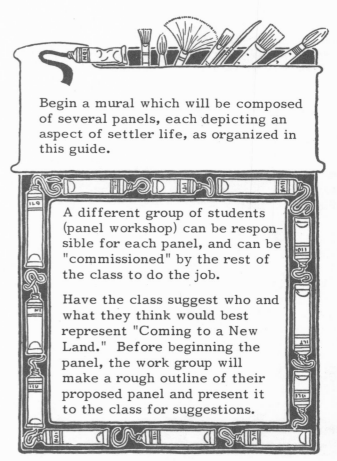

Begin a mural which will be composed of several panels, each depicting an aspect of settler life, as organized in this guide.

A different group of students (panel workshop) can be responsible for each panel, and can be "commissioned" by the rest of the class to do the job.

Have the class suggest who and what they think would best represent "Coming to a New Land." Before beginning the panel, the work group will make a rough outline of their proposed panel and present it to the class for suggestions.

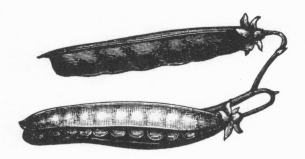

FUN WITH SEEDS

The Stell family planted corn, peas, squash, carrots, and pumpkins.

Corn and peas **are** the seeds.
Squash and pumpkins **contain** the seeds.
But where are the carrot seeds?

Children can investigate the seeds we eat, and the seeds in the food we eat. Teach the growth and development of seeds.

"I WENT TO THE LAND"

Play this memory game. The first player says, "I went to settle the land and took with me some rope." Each player in turn repeats the sentence and adds one more item. How long can you make the sentence before someone forgets an item?

A LONELY LIFE AND A HARD ONE

The life of the settlers was hazardous and beset with problems.

Some of these were:

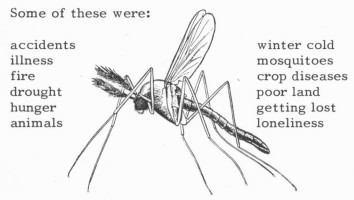

accidents
illness
fire
drought
hunger
animals

winter cold
mosquitoes
crop diseases
poor land
getting lost
loneliness

Discuss why and how these could be problems. What preventive measures were possible?

To illustrate some of these problems, read the class the stories, "The Bear Break-in," pp. 16-17, and "Fire," pp. 14-15, in **Early Family Home.**

Discuss the nature of the dangers, and such issues as why Susannah didn't cry out for help.

Read "Caught in a ring of fire," **Early Settler Storybook,** pp. 8-11.

Both Susannah Moodie in the previous story and the settler mother in this one are described as being in shock. Discuss the meaning of "shock," and its effects. Add it to the list of "feeling" words.

The young lady in this story can be considered a heroine. Other examples of heroic behavior are demonstrated in **Early Settler Storybook,** pp. 4-7.

Discuss the concept of heroism as it relates to settler lives and aspirations, not only in rescue situations. Are there heroes and heroines in the students' family profiles? Have students write or tell about "my family hero/heroine."

BABY, IT'S COLD OUTSIDE

The early pioneer way of life was closely affected by the environment.

Discuss or write about the ways in which our way of life is affected by the physical environment, whether rural or urban. Factors to consider include climate and physical surroundings.

How would your life be different if you lived in a much warmer place? — A much colder place?

How might your life be different if you lived near the ocean? — Near mountains? — On the plains?

Students might create a cartoon to depict some aspect of environmental influence, either for modern times or settler times.

TWO SIDES OF A COIN

While the environment presented many challenges to the settlers, it also provided them with many of their needs.

Make comparisons between:

How the Environment Helped
How the Environment Hindered

This activity may coordinate with natural science studies on the environment. Have students keep a journal, describing a week's activities. At the end of the week, they can summarize their impact on the environment: help or hindrance, and vice versa.

*This picture from **Early Village Life,** p. 4, shows a settler family alone on a Sunday. There is no church for worship and socializing. The first year in the new land was often difficult, both physically and emotionally. Hardship produced many of the virtues we associate with settler life.*

EARLY SETTLER BLUES

Note that the settlers were subject to many conditions over which they had no control. Examine and discuss this picture, reproduced from **Early Village Life,** p. 4.

What events and conditions could make life seem unbearable?

Why do you think the settlers did not give up?

Have students make up their own versions of the picture, adding speech balloons with suitable text.

CHEER UP

Creative writing topic:

A settler family has passed its first winter in the new land. Everyone is feeling lonely and discouraged. Write the family a letter of encouragement. Try to cheer them up.

This activity can teach or review the parts of the friendly letter. It will also contribute vocabulary for the "feelings" chart.

As a contrast, pupils will enjoy Mary's letter to her grandmother in **Early Farm Life,** pp. 15-16.

MAPS TELL A STORY

Have your students try to discover the nationalities of the first settlers in your area. (Use local history books, museums, interviews with historians, and visits to old cemeteries.)

On a large wall map, tack lengths of string to show the routes taken from the original homelands to your area. This activity can also be done by individuals using outline maps.

WORD STUDY

Each book in the series contains a glossary and an index. Here is an opportunity to introduce or review these tools.

Students may also begin booklets on early settler vocabulary studies, or an early settler dictionary for their own use.

They may add to these booklets colorful phrases and idioms such as the following from **The Early Family Home:**

p. 4   carve a new life
p. 7   lend a hand
p. 10   felling logs
p. 11   housewarming symbol
— and these compound words from p. 5 of **Early Village Life:** backwoods, homesick, newcomer, hardships, beadwork

Discuss:

Are there people today we could think of as pioneers?

Who would they be? Where would they be found?

Are there parts of the world that are still largely unsettled?

Use population distribution maps to determine the location of such areas.

Sometimes the term "pioneer" is used in the context of starting something new; for example, "He was a pioneer in computers." Ask your students if they have "pioneered" any new trends or ideas.

FURTHER RESEARCH

If it could be afforded, the settler was eager to buy a team of oxen. Why would oxen be preferred to horses?

The settler's first income was often from the sale of furs or potash. What is potash? How did the settlers get these goods? Why were they valuable commodities?

The first years.

Fifteen years later.

Thirty-five years later.

20

Chapter 2: A homestead grows

Objectives

Changes in the settler lifestyle as illustrated by the growth of the farmstead.

The impact of the environment on the early settler way of life (continued)

The practice of self-sufficiency in the settler way of life

Cooperation and resourcefulness among the settlers

Contents

- the growth of the homestead

- the settlers' first shanties or cabins

- keeping warm and dry

- the early farms: crops, harvest, livestock, tools

- the seasons in the settlers' life

- the building bee

Early Settler Series references

The Early Family Home
Early Loggers and the Sawmill
Early Village Life
Early Farm Life

Notes to the teacher

The students would profit from a visit to a pioneer home or farm before starting work on this unit.

Most resources dealing with the settler way of life tend to examine that lifestyle over a broad timespan and in varied regions of the country. Consequently, you and your students may discover differing, and at times conflicting, information. For example, "log cabin" may describe an early dirt-floored shanty or a well-constructed later home of several rooms.

It is suggested that you help your students become aware of these discrepancies and the reasons for their existence.

Encourage your students to use as many sources as possible in their research.

The Early Family Home, pp. 20-31
Early Village Life, pp. 8-9
Early Loggers and the Sawmill, pp. 8-9

THE CHANGING SCENE

These pictures from pages 4 and 5 of **The Early Family Home** show the changes in a simple homestead over a period of time.

Have groups of students examine the pictures to determine the nature and number of changes occurring. Which group can make the most comprehensive list?

A PLACE TO LIVE

Using the lists from the previous picture study as a beginning, extend the ideas. Construct a large chart as outlined below and have students use the following references as well as other sources to complete the comparison.

FIRST HOMES: SHANTY OR LOG CABIN

SIZE   usually around 16 ft. x 20 ft. (5m x 6m)

ROOMS   usually one room, perhaps a loft

MATERIALS   **Roof:** tree bark, saplings, hollow logs
Walls: rough logs, wooden pegs
Chinking: mud, wood chips
Windows: oiled paper or cloth
Doors: blanket

HEAT AND LIGHT   candles, oil lamps (sometimes), fireplaces of stones or mud, hole in roof for smoke, stone fireplace perhaps

FURNITURE   bunks built into walls, mattresses of boughs, table, benches, wooden pegs for clothes, a few wooden shelves

WATER SOURCE   springs, rivers, streams, lakes, wells (later)

DECORATIONS   rag rugs, cushions

LATER HOMES: LOG HOMES OR PLANK HOMES

SIZE   much larger, often two storys; basements and porches often added

ROOMS   parlor, kitchen, dining room, "borning" room, and other bedrooms

MATERIALS   **Roof:** cedar shingles
Walls: logs or wooden planks, nails
Chinking: strips of rags, cotton, paper and paste
Floors: smooth wooden floors
Windows: glass
Doors: proper doors and hinges

HEAT AND LIGHT   candles, kerosene lamps, iron cookstove, pipes to carry heat to other rooms

FURNITURE   cupboards, tables, chairs, beds, flop-benches

WATER SOURCE   rain barrel, cistern, wells, streams

DECORATIONS   paint made from ox blood or buttermilk and ocher, wallpaper, chimney pieces, furniture, more decorative rugs, cushions, curtains

The fireplace was the only source of heat for the home, and the settler family always gathered near it for warmth and companionship. This fireplace has a built-in seat; Grandma sits in the warmest spot.

When complete, discuss in terms of changes and improvements:

What conditions made it possible to build a better home?

(more time once land cleared and farm established; money made from selling farm produce available to buy tools; materials and some furniture; opening of a sawmill to make planks; availability of neighbors to help in the building)

Which improvements made life easier?
Which improvements made the home safer?
Which improvements do you think made the settlers the happiest?

Have students rank the improvements they would make in order of priority, giving reasons for their choices.

KEEPING WARM

Discuss the function and importance of the fireplace in the early settler home (see **The Early Family Home,** pp. 12-13).

The following also contributed to warding off chills and draughts:
— bedwarmers (usually heated rocks or bricks wrapped in cloth)
— hot water bottles (usually made of crockery

— foot-warmers (metal box filled with live coals)
— bear or buffalo skin robes
— quilts

Compare the above with present-day ways of keeping warm. Make a display (items, pictures, and articles) about "Keeping Warm: Then and Now." Individual students might make folders on the same theme.

HOW BIG WAS THAT?

Using string and a student standing at each corner, create a rectangle to represent the size of an average first home, approximately 16 ft. x 20 ft. (5m x 6m). This space could also be outlined on asphalt with chalk, or in poster paint on a washable floor. Emphasize that this was the family's total living space!

How many students can stand comfortably in the area?
How much furniture could you put in this space?

Have students construct a floor plan of the first cabin or shanty using a simple scale. Draw in items of furniture. This activity is easier if graph paper is used.

Review the story of Samantha Stell, **The Early Family Home,** pp. 7-11.

LIGHT MY FIRE

Page 13 of **The Early Family Home** stresses the importance of not letting the fire go out. The best method of getting it started again was to borrow a live coal from a neighbor, since there were no matches.

Other means of starting a fire were:

- tinderbox
- lens of an eyeglass or magnifying glass (need a sunny day)
- friction (rubbing sticks; this is tiring and time consuming)

Starting a fire on purpose is much simpler now. However, accidental fires are still a problem. Pupils may discuss how fires start accidentally and review fire safety.

BUCKET BRIGADE

Discuss fire-fighting methods then and now. The bucket brigade was used when the settlers had enough water and enough help to form a team. Have pupils try this as a game, using teams, teaspoons of water, and a cup (to save water). One member fills the spoon. The filled spoon must be passed from hand to hand. The last team member empties it into a cup. The first team to fill their cup wins a suitable reward.

Pupils may research the history of the fire engine, fireboats, and modern methods of fighting forest fires. A visit to a fire hall should be planned. Interested pupils may discover the various myths about human beings receiving or stealing fire.

A ROOM FOR LIVING

While the parlor was a very special room (see **The Early Family Home**, pp. 26-27), in later homes, it was the kitchen that became the hub of family activity, the real "living" room.

Discuss:

Why would the settlers spend most of their time in the kitchen?
Does your family have a special room where

*they gather much of the time? Do you have
a favorite room?*

Have students construct parallel lists of the
attractions of the early kitchen and their
favorite room, connecting the similar features.
Example:

Early Kitchen	My Family Room
● biggest room	● bigger than kitchen
● mother worked here	● where television is
● most comfortable furniture	● softer furniture
● warmest room	● cosy room, neatness not as important

RAIN, RAIN, GO AWAY

The early settler was often at the mercy
of the elements. Have students suggest how
the following would contribute to discomfort,
even while the settler was indoors:

- wind (blowing through chinks, blowing out stuffing)

- rain (blowing in through cracks and roof)

- snow (blowing in through cracks and roof)

- heat (cabins with no ventilation or insulation)

*How would the inclement weather also make
it difficult to get work done?*

Compose early settler "invocations" to the
elements. Model these on the old verse "Rain,
rain, go away!"

DOWN ON THE FARM

Once some land was cleared and a home built,
the settler was able to begin farming in earnest.
Under the following headings, have students
predict what they think might be involved.
Compare each step to what they know about
farming and gardening today.

The ground was often very hard and full of
rocks, roots, and stumps. It was broken up
using a hoe, mattock, or harrow. Once enough
stumps were removed, the farmer could use
oxen and a plow. A harrow leveled the ground
for planting.

*What happens if the soil is not properly
prepared?*

SOWING SEED

The farmer's main crops included grain (oats,
wheat, barley, rye, and corn). The seed was
planted by "broadcasting" or scattering, and
was left to be washed into the ground by
the rains. Corn was planted in "hills" much
as we plant it today. Other seeds were sown
in rows or planted individually.

*Why would wheat be such an important crop?
Who besides the family had to be fed?*

TENDING THE CROPS

Drought and insects were the two main
problems plaguing the settlers; there was
little defence against either. In addition,
they had to cope with cold weather and plant
diseases. Keeping the weeds down was a
never-ending task. Refer to **Early Farm
Life,** pp. 6-7 and 60-61 (locusts) and sky signals
on page 26.

*How would you feel if you lost your entire
crop to grasshoppers or drought? What could
this mean to the settlers?*

(It could mean a long hungry winter if the
settlers had no cash reserves or helpful
neighbors; possibly the farm would have to
be sold or abandoned.)

Stress the dependence of the settlers on a
successful crop.

A VEGETABLE GARDEN

Vegetables that were easy to grow and store for the winter were planted. Onions, peas, beans, carrots, cabbage, turnips, pumpkins, and potatoes were popular.

What were the settlers' methods of storing vegetables and fruit? How is food "stored" today?

OTHER CROPS

Other important items included an herb garden, fruit (apples were common), and flax (for making linen).

What would herbs be used for?
How long does it take an apple tree to grow before it produces fruit?

THE HARVEST

Grain was cut using a sickle or scythe. Later, a cradle cut grain and deposited it in neat bundles for easier gathering.

As the grain was gathered, it was bundled into sheaves and dragged to the barn where it was threshed, separating the grains from the straw.

It was spread out on the floor and hit with a flail. Next, the grain had to be separated from the chaff (little bits of seed head) by winnowing, putting it on a tray and shaking it in the wind so that the chaff, which was lighter than the grain, would blow away. The grain was then ready for grinding into flour.

Although there was so much hard work to be done, why was the harvest such a happy time for the settlers?

Using a flail to thresh wheat.

A SEASONAL APPROACH

Refer to **Early Farm Life**, pp. 18-19, "The first season on the farm." Settler life, particularly for those who farmed, was very much regulated by the seasons. Have students prepare a seasonal activity guide for the early settlers. See the checklist of suggestions in **Early Farm Life**, p. 28.

SPRING	SUMMER	FALL	WINTER
plow the ground	weed	cut grain	mend tools

As the students progress in early settler studies this guide can be expanded:

SPRING: sugaring, shearing, dyeing, spinning, weaving, planting, animal babies are born

SUMMER: harvesting flax (July) and other vegetable crops, berry-picking

FALL: making linen and linsey-woolsey, slaughtering, preserving, pickling

WINTER: lumbering

Daily chores for the settler family can also be investigated and added:

- cooking and baking
- raking ashes
- wood cutting as needed
- doing dishes, fetching water
- feeding and milking cows twice a day
- mending clothes
- gathering eggs

WHAT DO YOU DO ABOUT ...?

Invite a farmer or knowledgeable gardener to visit the class. Interview this person about crops and modern gardening or farming techniques. Have students prepare the interview questions ahead of time. It would be helpful and courteous to send your visitor this list of questions before the visit.

Your local paper may have an "Advice to gardeners" column. Students may write to the columnist with their questions, or watch the column for relevant queries. Start a clipping collection.

LIVESTOCK

The animals raised by the settlers were useful in many ways:

- oxen and horses for work
- horses and dogs for transportation
- pigs, cows, sheep, poultry for food
- sheep for wool

The livestock had to be fed, cared for, sheltered, and kept safe from wild animals. Oxen and pigs were among the first animals to be obtained by the settler.

Discuss:

If you could have only two animals as a settler, which two would you choose and why?
Why would the settler be reluctant to have pets?

Have the students match the following animals with their uses:

Animal	Uses
horse	meat, fat
goose	blankets, meat
chicken	wool, meat
sheep	work, transportation
oxen	eggs, meat
buffalo	work, transportation
pig	feathers, food

NOW WE'RE SPECIALIZED!

The early settlers' farm was a mixed economy farm. Today's farms tend to be specialized. Discuss why this change has come about. Research the types of farms found today. If the students become knowledgeable enough, consider debating the merits of the large specialized farm as opposed to the smaller mixed farm.

When the farmers could build a barn as beautiful as this one, they knew they had achieved success. Many old barns were an expression not only of farmers' ingenuity, but also of their sense of beauty.

FARM BUILDINGS

The first shanty often became the settlers' first barn. Later, a better and larger barn could be built, often of squared logs. Other buildings included a root cellar for storing root crops.

Before the settlers could build a barn, how would the animals be protected?
How did planting crops contribute to the farmer's self-sufficiency?
What changes have made farming more reliable today?

A REAL BARN RAISER

Barns and larger homes could not be built by one family alone. Consequently, all the family's friends and neighbors would form work parties to help build the framework for the house or barn. This event was called a "bee." Refer to **The Early Family Home**, pp. 48-49, **Early Village Life**, p. 43, and **Early Farm Life**, pp. 24-25.

What words describe the settler's attitudes to their neghbors? (try to elicit such terms as helpful, cooperative, reliable)
How were the settlers dependent on one another?
What tasks today are more easily done through the cooperation of a group?

Have students write about this topic, and compare their efforts. Plan a classroom "bee" to accomplish a task, either for the benefit of the class, school, or a worthy cause. Finish with a "social." (See the **Early Family Home**, pp. 44-45, and **Early Pleasures and Pastimes**, pp. 20-21.)

Discuss:

Do modern neighbors help each other as much as the settlers did?

Watch the newspapers, especially local papers, for news items dealing with neighborhood and community cooperation: eg. Block Parents, Neighborhood Watch, street parties.

Can your students devise a project that they, as good neighbors, could do for a worthy cause?

The settlers used whatever materials were available to build homes and barns. Find out about the materials used by the early settlers in your area or in other areas. For example, the prairie settler made sod homes or dugouts.

Those near river basins could incorporate stone and clay for mortar.

28

Use a green wash, dark crayons, or markers to create a dense forest on paper. Make sure the paper is totally covered.

Cut out black silhouettes of the early settlers and their first shanty or their farm. Superimpose these over the forest. Give the picture a title.

A WORK OF ART

Have students add a panel to the mural begun in Chapter 1. Depict an aspect of the settler home or farm.

A MODEL FARMSTEAD

Create a model of an early homestead. Begin by creating the "land" using a sand table or salt/flour relief on a large cardboard or wood base. Add buildings (cabins, outbuildings, barn, animal pens), and other items (fences, stumps, corduroy roads, woodpile, haystack, clothesline, carts). Create models of people and livestock.

Note: Collect small boxes which can be painted or covered with paper to represent buildings. See **The Early Family Home** pictures in this chapter.

A model of an early homestead can include everything from the house to the haystack.

SETTLERS' SEARS

Once settlers had a bit of spare cash, they liked, when possible, to purchase ready-made items. Have students construct an "Early Settler Catalog" of items for sale. Sections in the catalog might be as follows:

Furniture
Farm Tools
Kitchen Utensils and Implements
Clothing

Begin with the sections of Furniture and Farm Tools. The others may be completed later in the study, as appropriate.

While this activity may be done by individuals, it would be simpler to have small groups assume the responsibility for several items, which could be researched, illustrated, and described. It would be helpful to examine a few catalogs first in order to become familiar with the format and writing style. The **Early Settler Life Series** is packed with pictures of furniture, clothing, and farm tools. Have your students carefully research the art before they draw their own catalog items.

Some suggestions for items to include:

Furniture:

washstand	armchair
dry sink	trundle bed
dish dresser	candle stand
corner cupboard	side table
rocking chair	wall shelves
rope bed	flop bench
armoire	cradle
apothecary cabinet	side chair
desk	jack bed
blanket box	wig cabinet
bonnet box	dough box

Farm Implements and Tools:

flail	piggin
sickle	yoke
scythe	harness
plow	axes
harrow	cradle
seed drill	awl
stump puller	adze
hoe	quern
sap bucket	wet stone
water bucket	

A TREE MOBILE

Construct a "mobile" to illustrate aspects of the early settler homestead. Items might be drawn or colored, and then cut out to illustrate a front and back view of the particular item. Hang from the ceiling, windows, or even from a tree branch.

Some items to include: cabin, outbuildings, barn, woodpile, well implements, farm animals, and stumps.

DIORAMA

Have students, individually or in groups, construct a diorama to depict the interior of an early cabin or one of the rooms in the later home. Large cardboard boxes do well for this.

Before beginning, have students collect found materials from which to construct furnishings and features: wood scraps, pebbles, fabric scraps, twigs, etc.

If making a cabin, the outside of the box can be painted or decorated to resemble the cabin's exterior.

HOMESTEAD FOR SALE

After establishing a homestead, a settler family has decided to sell their farm and land.

Why might they wish to sell?

Have students create a newspaper advertisement or handbill designed to sell the farm.

How will you make your farm sound appealing? What will prospective buyers want to know? What features will you give special emphasis?

TREE STUDY

The Early Family Home names the following trees: elm, oak, ash, hemlock, pine, cedar, willow, walnut, butternut.

- Teach the growth of a tree.
- Make a bark and/or winter bud collection.
- Study deciduous and coniferous trees, their seeds and cones.
- Identify the uses of hard wood and soft wood.
- If possible, obtain a slice of tree trunk or visit the site of a stump.
- Locate and count the annual rings; how old is the tree?
- What events were happening when this old tree was 2, 3 (etc.) years old?

SPATTERWORK

Make leaf prints using the spatter technique. Scatter a variety of leaves over plain newsprint. Prepare an assortment of liquid paints. Have the children dip old toothbrushes into the colors, one color at a time. Hold the brush over the leaves, bristle side down. "Spatter" the paint over the leaves by drawing a tongue depressor or twig along the bristles towards your body. The paint will spatter away from you onto the leaves.

Have students mix their own colors:

red and yellow   = orange
black and white = grey
red and white   = pink
black and yellow = olive
red and blue   = purple
red and green   = brown
green and yellow = chartreuse

How does nature make beautiful leaf colors? Study the seasons of a leaf.

This "settler" village has been reconstructed. Notice the full-grown trees, split-rail fences, hitching posts, and "driveways."

Chapter 3: The village established

Objectives

The need for cooperation and sharing among the early settlers

The growth of community spirit

How and why villages became established

Site as a factor in developing villages

Establishing a context for local history studies

Contents

● neighborliness among the early settlers

● the concept of community spirit

● sites of early communities

● the settlers' need for grist mills

● components of a typical early village

● local community history

Early Settler Series references

Early Village Life
The Early Family Home

This would be an excellent time to consider a visit to an original or reconstructed village or settlement if there is one in your locality.

LOVE THY NEIGHBOR

Early settler life was lonely and isolated, but as more and more people arrived in an area, community spirit soon developed. The settlers needed each other.

Discuss "community spirit" and what it means to the students. This may require a look at communities first.

A community can be:

- a club
- a neighborhood
- a classroom
- a school
- a country
- the whole world

People can be members of many types of communities at the same time. Have students identify those to which they belong, and write a sentence about their role in each.

The early settlers had more limited communities. They had only family and their neighbors. Many tasks were shared for the good of everyone. Many joys were shared with the entire community.

Present the following statements or sayings for thought and discussion. Refer to **Early Village Life,** p. 7.

- Lend a hand
- Life is easier if you share resources, work, and good times
- My house is your house
- A friend in need is a friend indeed
- Love thy neighbor

Have students select a saying or statement that reflects one of the above examples, or a statement of their own community feeling from one of the above groups to which they belong. Have them produce that statement on art paper, using original ways of making their letters (ribbon, calico, cardboard, twigs, foil, gift wrap, etc.). Make illustrations to surround the letters.

GOOD NEIGHBORS

If you consider it appropriate, extend the ideas to doing a good deed for a neighbor. Have students suggest simple tasks that they might do:

- cutting grass, weeding, raking leaves
- helping with a younger child
- running an errand
- remembering to turn down the radio or TV when the windows are open, and also at night

COMMUNITY SPIRIT

Collect a file of newspaper articles dealing with neighborly happenings, community projects, etc. Assemble to form a bulletin board on "Community Spirit."

For each letter in the above words, have students find words or expressions to describe some aspect of early settler community life. This will be easiest if students work in small groups, later sharing their results.

Make a bulletin board display of the joint collection of words.

A GRINDING TASK

(Have students find out beforehand the amount of flour required to make one loaf of bread.)

Show students a cup full of grain. (Wheat or barley seeds, if available; if not, use corn.) Have them suggest ways they could grind this into flour.

If possible, bring a mortar and pestle and have students grind the grain, or try using two stones with relatively flat sides.

Discuss:

How much grain would have to be ground to made enough flour for just one loaf of bread?
How long do you think it would take to grind enough flour for a family's daily needs?
Whose job do you think this was?

Establish that grinding grain for flour was a laborious and time-consuming task for the settlers. Have students predict what would happen if someone moved into the area and established a grist mill where families could take their grain to be ground.

Pages 7 and 16, **Early Village Life,** refer to the gristmill owner, the sawmill owner and the general store owner as the pioneers of early village life.

"MAY I BORROW YOUR QUERN, MRS. JONES?"

Have students create a cartoon strip called "Neighbors — Early Settler Style," depicting relations between two or three fictitious neighboring families.

A WORK OF ART

Add a new panel to the mural begun in Chapter 1. Consider an early village street scene or a depiction of a work bee.

A quern.

A TYPICAL VILLAGE

Have students predict the components of an early village and compare their predictions to the following which were often found in the early villages and towns:

gristmill	blacksmith's shop
sawmill	cooper's shop
general store	bank
inn	harness-maker's shop
doctor's office	homes
print shop	

Compare the services available in the students' own community.

Discuss:

Which are still relevant today?
Which have disappeared and why?
What could the settlers have done if a particular service was not available?

Construct maps or models of a typical early village.

a) Maps — have students create simple maps, devising their own symbols and legend.

b) Models — Working in a small group, construct a model of a village. A large cut-down cardboard carton or heavy cardboard would make a good base. Use small boxes painted or covered with paper for buildings. Older students might later draw scale maps of their models.

NOTE: Have students begin early to collect "found" materials to use in their construction, eg. fabric scraps, boxes, and wood scraps.

FLOUR TODAY

What grains are commonly ground into flour today?

Have students bring bread bags and wrappers to school, to compose a composite list.

Visit a local supermarket or grocery store to discover the types of flour sold: rye, rice, and potato. Discover the special uses of each.

WHAT'S IN A NAME?

Refer to **The Early Family Home**, pp. 20-21.

The site of early settlements was often associated with water. (Trade and travel routes, sites of mills.) Villages were often named for these sites. Have students search a road map of their local area and assemble a list of place names which suggest water, eg. Brown's Mill, Red River, Harper's Dam.

From the name, what type of water would you expect to find?

WATER MAKES THE WHEELS GO ROUND

Assemble students around a water tap. Have a small strip of cardboard (not too rigid) approximately 1½" x 5" (3cm x 12cm). Have students predict what will happen if this strip is held beneath the tap and the water is turned on. Do this, experimenting with various water pressures.

What caused the strip to deflect?
What do we call this form of energy?

Have students predict what would be possible if a series of strips were assembled to form a wheel. (The water would turn the wheel which could then make grinding stones turn.)

Examine the picture and text on p. 16 of **Early Village Life.**

Why did villages often grow up near the site of a mill?
Why did other businesses locate near the mill?
Where else did villages tend to become established? (at a crossroads, a harbor)
Why would this be the case?

Discuss expressions such as "keep your nose to the grindstone," "grist for the mill," "millstone around your neck," "milling around," "put through the mill," "run of the mill."

What are other ways of saying the same things?

How many Millers are there in your local phone directory? Have students speculate as to why this is still a common surname.

(Hundreds of years ago people had only one name. This became confusing. As time went by, people started adding descriptive terms to the first name to distinguish among people, eg. John the miller, John who lives over the hill. These eventually became John Miller or John Hill. Because virtually every village had a miller of one kind or another, we have many Millers today.)

Other common surnames may be noted as village studies progress: Smith, Carpenter, Potter, Cooper, Wainwright. These once denoted occupations.

Some villages were named for saints, explorers, or native people's terms and ideas. Find references to these.

Every community had its beginnings, often as a village. Find out how and when your community began. If feasible, take a walking tour of the original area.

Are there any original buildings still there?
Are there public monuments or markers to denote early sites, explorers, settlers?
What are the oldest buildings in your community?

Make a photographic or pictorial record of the buildings you visit. Add information and assemble into a "local history" book. Make a map of your walking tour.

Interview the oldest person you can find in your community. The whole class can assist in preparing the questions, while two or three others are selected to hold the interview. Tape the interview so that everyone can hear it.

Invite a local historian to visit the class. Collect local history books, pictures, and collections. Inquire at the local newspaper about obtaining a copy of one of their earliest papers.

MAPS TELL A STORY

Have students discover the nationalities of the first settlers in your specific area (using local history books, museums, interviews with historians). On a large wall map, tack lengths of string to show the routes taken from the original homelands to your area. This activity can also be done individually using outline maps.

ON THE STREET WHERE I LIVE

Have students make a map of their street, the school street, where their club meets, or the like. If there is an older resident or caretaker, who remembers how the street has changed, conduct an interview, and illustrate changes. Immigrant children and others who have moved may describe the differences between their former and present school, community, and routes.

MY KIND OF TOWN

Consider the degree of renown of your community. Does it have an exciting history? Does it have tourist attractions, or other centers and landmarks which you can visit and ensure that the pupils are aware of?

I GET AROUND

Have students map their route to school. Describe which bus routes, highways, or streets they take on a regular basis with the family, with friends, by themselves. Ask them to map the routes they can take alone. Have them tell where they want to go when they are older, within the community, the country, the world. What do they know about these places? What do they imagine about them?

Chapter 4: Homespun

Objectives

The self-sufficiency and resourcefulness of the early settlers with respect to providing for everyday needs around the home.

An understanding and appreciation of the settlers' industry and capacity for work, as shown by the time-consuming tasks that were required to provide for the simple needs.

Early Settler Series references

Early Village Life
The Early Family Home
Early Pleasures and Pastimes
Early Health and Medicine

Notes to the teacher

This chapter's objectives will be best accomplished if the students have some opportunity to become involved in actually doing activities and making the various items. The activities require some preparation and thought beforehand on the part of the teacher with respect to finding and collecting materials and supplies.

Contents

- settler self-sufficiency
- fabrics and clothing: spinning, dyeing, weaving, knitting, clothing styles
- functional items from scraps: braiding, hooking, quilting
- keeping clean; laundry
- candlemaking
- decorative arts: stencils dried flowers
- making dolls
- health care practices, home remedies, folk medicine

SETTLER SELF-SUFFICIENCY

The self-sufficiency of the early settlers has been discussed in chapter one. You might like to recall that discussion.

Nowhere was settler ingenuity more evident than in the home. Present students with the following piece of advice which is taken from an early cookery book:

NEVER WASTE OR THROW AWAY ANYTHING THAT CAN BE TURNED TO ACCOUNT

What is meant by "turned to account"?
Why would this be a particularly good piece of advice?
Is this advice followed by everybody today?
Why not?

Have students keep a list for a two-day period of everything they waste or throw away. Discuss the lists:

How many are careless or wasteful?
How would they have to change their habits if they were early settlers?

THE CLOTHES ON THEIR BACKS

When it came to making clothing, the settlers had to use whatever resources were available or could be grown. Basically they were limited to leather and furs (made from animal hides), wool (from sheep), linen (from the flax plant), and some purchased cotton.

To illustrate how the settlers were limited in the fabrics available to them, collect scrap pieces of fabric in wool, linen, cotton, and leather. Draw and cut two oversized cardboard "paper dolls", one male, one female, and make "clothing" for them, cutting out the appropriate shapes and gluing them to the figures. Pictures from throughout the Early Settler Series will illustrate the clothing styles.

The best way to understand just how much was involved in the production of a piece of cloth is to examine one process step-by-step, trying out the activities where feasible.

FROM FLEECE TO YARN

You will need to obtain some raw sheep fleece. This is often available from craft shops or weaving supply stores. Local spinning and weaving associations can usually direct you to the nearest source. The fleece may be already washed or may be still "in the grease" (the natural oils still in the fleece; this is easier to work with).

Gently pull the fleece apart so that the accumulated seeds and grasses which stick to the fleece fall. Then the wool must be carded or untangled. Wooden paddles with small nails, called carders, are used for this.

You may be able to purchase or borrow a pair. If not, untangle and straighten the fleece as best you can (a wire dog brush would be helpful).

Distribute a small piece of fleece to each student. Instruct students to pull out the fleece into a long thick thread. What happens if you pull too much? Now try twisting each thread until it resembles a piece of string. What happens now if the thread is pulled? It is this twist that gives the thread strength, and twisting the thread is the essence of the spinning process.

The fleece was spun into yarn using a variety of kinds of spinning wheels or using a drop spindle. A drop spindle can usually be purchased very reasonably in a weaving supply store. If possible, obtain a drop spindle and try some spinning. If there is a local spinning and weaving association, you may be able to contact a spinner who will come to your class and demonstrate the process. Most spinners are delighted to show off their skills.

Carding wool.

ADD A LITTLE COLOR

The next step in the process is dyeing the wool. (This may actually be done before or after spinning, but the wool must be well washed.) Use lukewarm water and a mild detergent. Handle the wool gently so as not to mat it, and rinse several times. Spread out on towels to dry. Even if you have not done any spinning, do try some dyeing; it's quite easy and plenty of fun!

Dyes came from nature. Roots, leaves, bark, nuts, flowers, and lichens were all sources of the subtle colors produced by natural dyes. The most colorful plants were not necessarily the source of the most vibrant dyes. Some surprisingly beautiful hues came from the most unlikely-looking plants.

Here is a good "recipe" to try using onion skins.

1. Simmer about 2 large handfuls of onion skins in about 1 gallon of water (or about 4 liters), preferably soft water, for about 45 minutes. Use an enamel or stainless steel pot. Strain off skins and discard.

2. Cool dye bath to hand heat and put in about 10 ounces (approximately 30 grams) of wool which has been wetted in water beforehand.

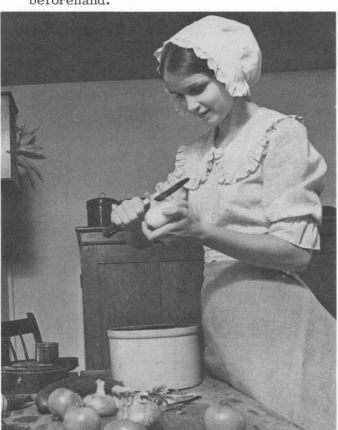

3. Slowly bring dye bath to a simmer. Simmer gently for about 15 minutes. Stir lightly with a wooden spoon, glass rod, a piece of doweling, or a paint stock.

4. Remove the yarn using the utensil from above and let drip over the dye bath. Insert into a pail of hot water, rinse, and squeeze gently. Then rinse again in cooler water and then squeeze again. Hang to dry in the shade. (You may wish to leave some wool in the dye bath and simmer longer; a darker shade will result.)

If you do not have wool, try dyeing some old white cotton. Synthetics will not take the dye.

USING A MORDANT

Dyeing becomes much more interesting when a mordant is added to the dye bath. A mordant is a chemical which alters the colors and improves color fastness. The most common mordants are alum and cream of tartar. (Alum is readily available in a drug store.) Mix 1½ tsp. alum and 1¼ tsp. cream of tartar together in a little boiling water and dissolve in the dye bath before adding wool. You might begin by repeating the onion-skin recipe, this time adding the mordants to see what happens.

FROM YARN TO FABRIC

Yarns were knit or woven into fabric. A piece of old knitting and a piece of loosely woven wool fabric can be pulled apart to examine how the yarn is interlocked to form a fabric.

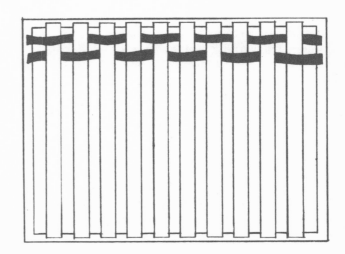

The simplest way to weave is using paper strips. Strips of colored paper are glued to a simple cardboard frame to form a warp, the lengthwise threads around which the other threads are woven. The weft, or crosswise, strips are then woven in and out of the warp strips, alternating under and over. Use different colors for warp and weft so that the pattern shows more clearly.

A simple weaving loom can be made by constructing a small wooden frame with rows of nails at the top and bottom around which the warp can be wound (very firmly). The nails should be about ½ inch (approximately 1cm) apart. The weft thread (a continuous thread wound around a piece of stiff cardboard which serves as a simple shuttle) is then woven back and forth in and out of the warp. A wide-toothed comb can be used after each row or two in order to "pack down" the weft threads.

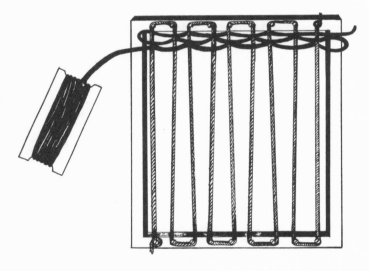

Hooked rugs were made using thinner strips of wool rags. Using a special hook, designs were hooked into the back of canvas or burlap. Rug-hooking kits or supplies are available and the craft is easy to learn. Perhaps someone has a hooked rug to bring to school for you to examine, or maybe someone knows a person who will come to class and demonstrate the technique.

BRAIDED RUGS

You may have to begin by teaching your students to braid. One way is to hang three strips of fabric (each in a different color) from a door handle and let students practice when other work is completed.

You may wish to make one large rug or have students make small individual rugs. This will depend on the amount of fabric you have.

One class became very ambitious and made themselves a braided rug large enough to put on the floor in their reading corner. They were very proud of their efforts.

Cut long strips of fabric approximately 1 inch (2.5cm) wide. Sew three strips of different colors together securely at one end. The sewn end will need to be placed under something heavy so that the strips can be held taut while being braided. One way is to put the end between a close-fitting door. Or, try sewing a fabric "jacket" around a rock. Pin material to be braided to the rock. When the braiding is complete, the strips must be sewn together at the raw end to keep them from coming undone. Try to keep the strips flat while braiding in order to get a nice neat braid. The braiding should be quite firmly done.

When a number of strips have been braided the rug may be started. The braid is coiled around itself. Sew the sides of each braid together as you go. Take care to keep the braids flat as you sew or you will end up with a rug that will not lie flat. At the end of each braid, sew in the tail end securely and attach another braid. The rug is finished when you reach the desired size.

COSY QUILTS

Scraps that were too short for rug making could be used to make a quilt. They were sewn together, usually in a pattern, to make one large top which was sewn to a back layer of soft wool or cotton fleece in between. Tiny neat quilting stitches held the three layers together. This work was done on a frame, often at a quilting bee where many hands could speed up the tedious work. (See **The Early Family Home,** pp. 46-47.)

Try to have a quilt brought to school to examine, preferably an old one if it is possible. Collect pictures of quilts from craft and homemaking magazines. (Many deal specifically with quilting.) Examine the various patterns and designs. Many have interesting names.

Some modern quilts depict scenes or episodes. Children may design a quilt as a memento of trips taken, each "block" representing a different trip.

Students who have babies in the family may wish to design and make crib quilts.

Quilted pot holders, placemats, coasters, trivets, and Christmas stockings are excellent items for a fund-raising bee and sale.

A simple quilt "block" (a section of patches) can be made fairly easily. Uniform squares of fabric (4 inches or 10cm is a good size) are cut out on the straight grain. After they are arranged into a design they are stitched together, first into rows and then into sections. A block will be 3 x 3 squares or 4 x 4 squares, etc. A number of blocks can be stitched together to make a large quilt top. Once the edges are hemmed, your quilt top will make an attractive wall hanging.

PAPER PATCHWORK

Cut various colored papers into squares and triangles of uniform size. (The triangles will be the squares cut in half.) Arrange these to form an attractive design, experimenting as much as possible before deciding on the design. Glue the paper pieces onto a backing and give each patchwork design a name. (It will be easier if students limit their designs to two or three colors.)

MAKING DOLLS

An early settler mother, grandmother, or older sister would take great pleasure in making a simple doll for a young child. Try making one or more dolls by the following methods:

TIN–CAN DOLLS

Simple dolls can be made from paper maché and old tin cans, and then dressed as early settlers.

1 Make paper maché balls about 4 inches (10cm) in diameter. Make the final layer of pink tissue. When dry, paint or draw eyes, nose, and mouth on the ball, which has now become a head. Yarn or string "hair" may be glued on. A bonnet or hat may be made if desired.

2 An empty tin can will become the doll's body. Clothing, made from scrap fabrics, is glued onto the can. Female dolls are the easiest to fashion. Arms made from fabric can be glued onto each side.

3 Place the "head" onto the top of the can. It should just fit inside the rim. If it is a bit too small, build up the bottom with several layers of masking tape. Do not attach the head permanently as it may be turned or lowered to change the doll.

3

1

2

CLOTHESPEG DOLLS

Old style wooden clothespegs are still available at craft shops. Simple dolls are made by painting faces at the top of the peg, adding yarn or string hair and gluing on scraps of fabric to make simple clothing. Usuallly there were no arms.

CORN-HUSK DOLLS

You will need to save a supply of corn husks in order to make these dolls. Raffia, which is available at craft shops, would make a suitable substitute.

1 If you are using dried corn husks, use only the smooth inner leaves. Cut away the pointed tips and stiff stems. Soak the husks in warm water for 15 minutes before using. (These must be kept damp while they are being worked with.)

2 Take a length of raffia or several long husks and tie together at the top (using a strong thread).

3 Distribute husks or raffia over a roll of husk or raffia to form a head.

4 Cut a short length of raffia or several husks (for arms) and put between the front and back layers.

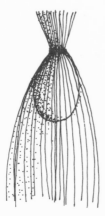

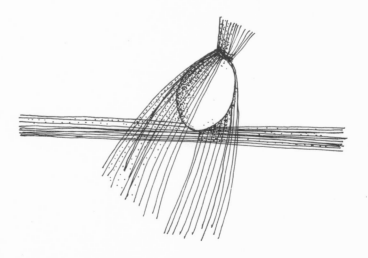

5 Take a length of raffia (single strand) or a narrow piece of husk and wrap around the waist and neck of the doll to hold it together, crossing over the chest. Go round several times and secure.

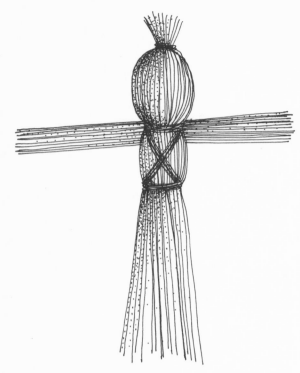

6 Tie ends of arms.

7 For a boy doll, separate and tie legs.

8 The dolls may be dressed in early settler style by making simple clothing.

APPLE DOLLS

A very simple version of the apple doll may be made as follows.

1 Peel an apple (preferably a firm one) and insert a popsicle stick up through the middle.

2 Using a small knife, cut a face by hollowing a place for each eye, and cutting away part of the apple to leave a nose and mouth. Make these rather large to allow for shrinkage.

3 Leave the apples to dry and shrivel for several days. They will darken considerably.

4 When the apples have dried, the faces may be finished. Tiny glass-head pins stuck in the apple make excellent "eyes." Yarn, thread, or best of all, fleece, may be glued on to make hair.

5 Glue "paper doll" style clothing to the popsicle stick which makes a simple body for the doll.

SEWING A FINE STITCH

When early settler girls made samplers, they not only learned to do fine embroidery work, they also learned their numbers and alphabet letters. Once they became accomplished at the various stitches used (chain, satin, blanket, outline, and cross stitches), they could stitch pictures, poems, prayers or Bible passages onto the linen background.

To make simple samplers you will need embroidery thread and needles, a suitable fabric such as linen, or an even, not too tightly woven, cotton. A craft shop or needlework shop will have the best materials. Try just one kind of stitch or the cross stitch and keep the pattern simple, perhaps limiting the sampler to the alphabet and the numbers.

Everyday clothes: plain dress, bonnet, and apron

RIGHT IN FASHION, SETTLER STYLE

Clothing styles for the early settlers varied with the period, the economic status of the family, and the type of life led. Fashion-conscious students today will find it difficult to comprehend that most settlers had but two sets of clothes, one for everyday, and one for Sunday-best.

Discuss:

How would you have to treat your clothes if you only had two outfits?
Would style have been as important to the settlers as it is to some people today? Why?/Why not?
Why were aprons such a good idea?
Would clothes have looked as clean and neat as today? Why not?
If you could only have two outfits, what would they be?

Many clothing styles appear in the pictures throughout the Early Settler Series books. Have each student choose one illustrated outfit and make a picture of a person wearing the outfit. Include both adults and children.

Keep the figures in the picture to a standard size of about 18 inches (45cm). Cut each figure out and paste onto a piece of light cardboard. Affix a stand to the back of each figure and display the figures in a group. Give your display a title. How about "Early Settler Fashion Parade?"

KEEPING CLEAN

Before one could even think about washing or doing laundry, the soap had to be made. It is not recommended that you make soap with your students, as one of the basic ingredients, lye, is very caustic. How soap was made is outlined on pp. 40-41 of **The Early Family Home.**

Doing the laundry was quite a task — no throwing a load in the automatic washer. Present students with the following outline of how to wash a load of clothes. Later have them write a step-by-step set of instructions for doing laundry today. Try to estimate how long it must have taken to do a load of washing early settler style.

How to Wash Clothes

1 Build a fire in the backyard and heat a kettle of rainwater.

2 Set tubs so smoke won't blow in your eyes if the wind is pert.

3 Shave a whole cake of lye soap into the boiling water.

4 Sort things into 3 piles, 1 white, 1 colored, and 1 for work britches and rags.

5 Stir some flour in cold water until smooth, then thin down with boiling water (starch).

6 Rub dirty spots on a board. Scrub hard. Then boil.

7 Rub colored things but don't boil. Just rinse and starch.

8 Take white things out of the kettle with a broomstick. Then rinse, blue, and starch.

9 Spread tea towels on the grass.

10 Hang old rags on the fence.

11 Pour rinse water on the flower beds.

12 Turn tubs upside down.

13 Put on clean clothes, comb your hair, put your feet up and rest awhile.

Ask if someone has an old scrub board which can be brought to school. Try washing some really dirty rags by hand.

THIS LITTLE LIGHT OF MINE

When your students find out how long it took to make candles in early settler days, they will appreciate the convenience of electric lights.

A young girl shares her feelings about candle-making on p. 39 of **The Early Family Home.** Read the paragraph that she has written. Have each student choose a "hateful chore" and write a paragraph about it. Exchange paragraphs among students. Have each write a paragraph of advice to the other on how to make the particular hateful chore less hateful.

Candles were usually made from tallow (left-over animal and vegetable fats). Sometimes a little beeswax or bayberry wax might be added to the tallow. Pure beeswax or bayberry candles were kept for special occasions.

There were two basic methods: dipping the candle wick into the melted tallow or pouring it into molds. Page 38 of **The Early Family Home** illustrates both methods. The tallow had its problems; it burned unevenly, melted in the summer (which is why many candlesticks were tubular in design), and was appealing to mice. Around 1860 paraffin wax replaced the use of tallow.

Try some candle dipping. Tallow is usually available from meat-packing companies, although paraffin will do. Butcher string will make adequate wicks. Candlewicking, available in many craft shops, will burn better.

Melt the tallow in deep containers (large juice tins are just right) which have been placed in a pot of heated water.

Tie several pieces of candlewicking to a sturdy piece of branch or piece of doweling. Gently dip the wicks into the tallow and hang them to dry. Make sure to put paper under the dripping candles to catch the drips.

After the tallow hardens, the candle can be dipped again. It takes a number of dippings before enough tallow accumulates on the wick. Try to do your dipping in a cool room so that the tallow will harden before it all drips off the wick.

Once you have a tallow candle, make a comparison of the qualities of the tallow candle, an ordinary paraffin candle, and candles made of bayberry and beeswax (usually available at gift shops). Burn one of each simultaneously and compare for length of burn, odor, smoke produced, light cast, and messiness.

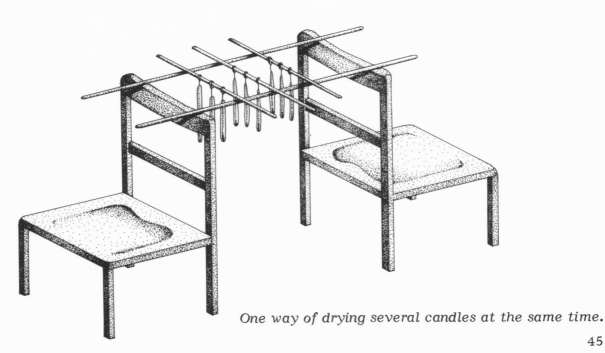

One way of drying several candles at the same time.

LANTERNS

When carried outdoors, candles quickly blew out. Lanterns were often made out of metal and would be punched full of holes so that light could shine out. You will need to save up some empty juice cans and their cut-off lids.

1 Laying the can on one side, make little holes all over the can by piercing the sides with a sharp nail and a hammer. It is particularly effective to make a design of the holes. Make holes in the lid too. (You will need to rest the lid between two blocks of wood.)

2 Fasten the lid to the can on one side by threading a piece of thin wire through a hole in the lid and a hole at the top of the can. Close the wire with pliers. The lid must be able to move up and down. Now do the same thing on the other side of the can.

3 A wire handle may also be affixed to the top of the can.

4 Put a small candle in the bottom of the lantern and let your light shine out!

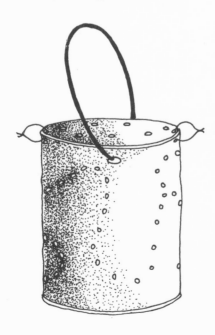

DECORATING WITH WILDFLOWERS

Garden and wild flowers were dried, pressed, and made into pictures, or used to decorate various items. Press some flowers and leaves between pieces of paper toweling placed under a heavy weight (a pile of books does very well). Make pictures, a greeting card, or notepaper by arranging the flowers in a design and gluing with a thinned mixture of white glue onto the background.

A POTPOURRI

A potpourri is a mixture of dried flower petals, herb leaves, and fruit peels which provide a pleasant scent. Often the mixture was sewn into a sachet and placed in a drawer or closet to provide a fresh fragrance. Potpourris can be purchased today in gift shops. Purchase samples of several varieties. What ingredients can be identified?

THE DECORATIVE ARTS

While there wasn't much time or energy left for decorating and enhancing everyday items, the settlers did their best, using simple materials and techniques. Wooden ware was often carved, fabrics were spruced up with needlework, and painted items were often decorated with freehand artwork.

STENCIL DESIGNS

These were relatively easy to use and did not require a great deal of skill. They were applied in many places: bare floors, furniture, especially chair backs, trays, spice tins, and boxes. Shapes were cut out of heavy cardboard and discarded, leaving the remaining stencil as a template. The shapes were then traced onto the surface in any combination. The color was filled in while the stencil was in place or after it had been removed.

Try making stencils and decorating some items: boxes, pieces of wood, a piece of classroom equipment. Stenciled strips of cardboard would make an attractive border around the chalkboard or a door. The above are some typical designs. Books on early furniture will provide other ideas.

Cups were community property!

SHARING THEIR GERMS

The early settlers knew much less about medicine than we know today. Present students with the following statements about health care and practices. Discuss each with respect to the problems which might have resulted from each practice and what would be done today in the same situation.

- Often many people drank from the same cup and used the same dishes.
- Inns would have one towel, comb, and wash bowl to be shared by all the guests. Strangers were often required to share beds.
- People did not bathe very often because bathing was believed to wash away body oils.
- People believed that body oils prevented illness.

- Dirty wash water was often thrown outside the door of the home. It seeped into a nearby well.
- A popular disease treatment was to take blood from people.
- Doctors did not sterilize their instruments before using them.
- Fresh air and water were believed to be harmful to sick people. Patients were kept in dark, stuffy rooms.

Information about early settler health practices can be found in **The Early Family Home**, pp. 32-33, **Early Village Life**, pp. 28-29, and **Early Health and Medicine**.

47

HOME REMEDIES

Often doctors were not available and many settlers tried to cure themselves at home. Plants, roots, and flowers were brewed into medicines. The herb garden was an important part of every homestead.

Following is a list of ailments on the left and "cures" on the right. Attempt to match the ailment and the remedy. This will be essentially a guessing exercise, but plenty of fun.

AILMENT	REMEDY
1 Frazzled nerves	a Rub with a mixture of sage and oil
2 A bleeding cut or wound	b Make a syrup of comfrey and honey
3 Aching joints	c Chew bark of willow tree
4 Sore eyes	d Apply sweet basil
5 Upset stomach	e Rub with horseradish juice
6 Aching feet	f Chew roots of nerve-vine
7 Cough	g Apply garlic to feet at night
8 Headache	h Apply fresh heliotrope leaves
9 Indigestion	i Drink thick violet tea
10 Wasp sting	j Drink hop tea
11 Cold	k Drink basil tea
12 Canker in the mouth	l Wash with cold camomile tea

ANSWERS
1 (f)　　7 (b)
2 (h)　　8 (c)
3 (a)　　9 (j)
4 (l)　　10 (d)
5 (k)　　11 (g)
6 (e)　　12 (i)

Are you glad you were born in the twentieth century?

48

FOLK MEDICINE

Folk cures, based mainly on superstition, were not uncommon beliefs in many rural communities. When presenting the following, take care that your students understand that the early settlers who used these cures were not lacking in intelligence. Rather, they did not have the benefit of the medical knowledge that is available to us today. When the pain or discomfort was great and no medical help was available, people cannot be blamed for trying anything!

Bad temper in a child pass the child's head through the left leg of its father's trousers

Dog bite take some hairs from the offending dog and place them on the wound

Freckles to prevent freckles rub a baby goose over the face

Sore back lie on the floor face down and have someone tread on the sore part

Rheumatism carry a horse chestnut in the pocket

Stitch in the side spit on a pebble and throw it over your shoulder

Sore mouth rinse with water from the blacksmith's forge

Sty rub the tail of a cat on the sty

Earache apply a poultice made from the wool of a black sheep

Toothache put a clove of garlic in the ear on the same side as the ache

Warts rub a piece of apple on the wart and blow on it at the same time

After discussing these "cures," try writing some contemporary "cures" for the same ailments.

Discuss:

Does the old expression "the cure is worse than the disease" apply in these cases? Which cures would actually have been harmful?

TAKE THE TEA CURE

Try some weak herbal teas (available in health-food stores, tea shops, and many fancy food shops). Since many were used as remedies for just about everything, everyone should be wonderfully well after trying the various teas.

Basil upset stomach

Heliotrope nerves, heart palpitations, aches and pains

Lemon Balm stomach ache, fever, chills, flu

Sage coughs, colds, indigestion, constipation

Mint chills, colds, headaches, bronchitis

Marjoram nerves, headaches

Rosehip lung congestion, constipation, colds, flu, measles

Chapter 5: Bread on the table

Objectives

Changes in the settlers' lifestyle as illustrated by the changes in their diet.

An appreciation of the difficulties faced by the settlers in meeting such a basic need as food.

The self-sufficiency and ingenuity of the settlers with respect to acquiring and preparing food.

How food acquisition and preparation has changed since settler days.

Early Settler Series references

Food for the Settler
Early Stores and Markets
Early Village Life

Contents

- sources of food before there were stores: fishing, hunting and trapping, gathering, planting, raising animals

- the help of the Indians

- food requirements for a hard day's work

- some common foods: berries, corn, herbs

- staples: bread and butter

- apples, an important commodity

- cooking methods; kitchen gadgets

- preserving food

- advertising food

- table manners

- sweets in the settler diet

- food from many countries

- food for special occasions

Notes to the teacher

Many of the activities suggested in this chapter involve cooking or some form of food preparation. Many recipes are included in **Food for the Settler.** You will not be able to try them all; do consider trying a few. This would be a good time to ask parents in to help. Asking students to contribute food items will help defray the costs involved.

You might consider having students choose favorite recipes. Copy these and assemble into an "Early Settler Recipe Book." Encourage students to take the book home and try some of the recipes.

Before having pupils cook and eat the suggested foods, teachers are advised to discover any dietary laws, customs, or allergies among the pupils, which might inhibit or preclude participation.

It is seldom advisable to question young children closely about family eating habits or the content of their meals. However, incidental lessons can be taught on:

- table settings
- food groups
- balanced meals
- nutritional concerns:
  breakfast foods
  snacks
  "fast foods"

Cooking provides a wealth of pleasant opportunities for discovering and developing skills in organization, measurement, cooperation, timing, sequence, judgement, and vocabulary development.

Prepare students for a degree of trial and error. Results from cooking at high altitudes vary from cooking at sea level. Oven temperatures also vary. Just as the author "tested and adapted" these recipes from early settler books, so can the students prepare to test their results as they go along. An activity which demands this kind of adaptability is understanding measurements which are found in some recipes:

    a dash
    a pinch
    a sprinkle
    a handful
    "to taste"

These ingredients are needed, but the amounts are inexact. They call for individual judgement and preference.

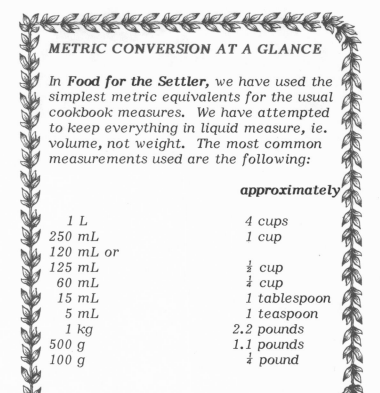

METRIC CONVERSION AT A GLANCE

In **Food for the Settler,** we have used the simplest metric equivalents for the usual cookbook measures. We have attempted to keep everything in liquid measure, ie. volume, not weight. The most common measurements used are the following:

	approximately
1 L	4 cups
250 mL	1 cup
120 mL or	
125 mL	$\frac{1}{2}$ cup
60 mL	$\frac{1}{4}$ cup
15 mL	1 tablespoon
5 mL	1 teaspoon
1 kg	2.2 pounds
500 g	1.1 pounds
100 g	$\frac{1}{4}$ pound

A LEG OF LAMB

Early settlers usually had to cope with an entire animal when planning meals. Now we can buy the cuts we want. Teachers may find this chapter appropriate for teaching the cuts of meat and their sources: bacon, ham, roasts, chops, ribs from hogs, cattle, lambs. A visit to a butcher shop may be planned to view the cuts in preparation.

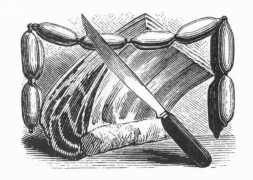

VOCABULARY STUDIES

All children can learn to recognize and use standard cooking terminology. The following is a list of the verbs found in the recipes in **Food for the Settler.** Many are also nouns in different contexts, and can provide practice in using homophones, eg. season of the year, season the stew.

sift	heat	brown
cut	dust	simmer
cover	strain	stuff
season	store	beat
slice	cut in	thicken
mix	sprinkle	shake
add	press	roll
stir	let rest	baste
remove	roll	skim
coat	preheat	soften
drain	spoon into	scald
mash	slit	blend
melt	bake	press
pour	wash	moisten
divide	remove	grease
grate	reduce	beat
serve	ladle	fold
garnish	seal	flute
fry	chop	slash
grate		

The following herbs, spices, and flavorings are used in the text and can provide opportunities for tasting and recognizing by sight and smell.

parsley	salt
savory	pepper
thyme	nutmeg
chives	sugar
onion	ginger
cayenne pepper	mace
marjoram	cinnamon
dry mustard	vanilla
paprika	cocoa
cloves	

LIVING OFF THE LAND

List on a chart the following methods used by the settlers to obtain food: **fishing, hunting and trapping, gathering, planting, raising animals.**

Brainstorm these methods: the foods obtained, additional information about the method and the people involved. Keep a list of any questions that arise.

Did the settlers have margarine?
Did they use a rod and reel?

Look for the answers as work on the subject of food progresses.

Divide students into five research groups. Each group is responsible for finding out more about one of the methods. Use **Food for the Settler** and any other material available. Refer to work on farming done during Chapter 2.

Fishing, pp. 6-9
Hunting and Trapping, pp. 10-17
Gathering, pp. 19-29
Planting, pp. 28-31
Raising Animals, pp. 32-35

Discuss:

What kind of skills were important to the settlers?
Would you like to live on their diet?
Why/Why not?
What foods would you miss most if you were a settler?
Was nature a friend, enemy, or both?
Why?
What does "self-sufficient" mean with respect to food?

Begin a mural, "Food for the Settler." Divide a large sheet of mural paper into 5 sections: Fishing, Hunting and Trapping, Gathering, Planting, and Raising Animals. Have each research group complete one section of the mural. Include pictures, information, recipes, and cartoons.

Why was it important to learn fishing skills quickly?

Create cartoons to illustrate some of these early fishing attempts. Include speech balloons.

Many of the early settlers were not experts when it came to such basic skills as fishing. Read "Fishing the Clumsy Way" in **Food for the Settler,** p. 6.

Why might some of the settlers not know how to fish?
Which method might work best?
Why would most of the methods not work?
Can you think of some other methods they might have tried?
Who helped the settlers learn better fishing methods?

THANKS TO THE INDIANS

The Indians were a great help to the early settlers; many settlers would not have survived the first winter without their help and advice. Have a group of students research the ways the Indians helped and the things they taught the early settlers. Make a presentation to the rest of the class.

SQUIRREL PIE? — NO THANKS!

Present the following quotation:

> "When we found it impossible to get any meat, the different kinds of squirrels supplied us with pies, stews, and roasts ... In a trap set for such 'small deer' (the name we called the squirrels) we often caught from ten to twelve a day."
> (**Food for the Settler,** p. 12)

Discuss:
Why was it sometimes necessary for the settlers to trap squirrels?
How do you think they felt about doing this?
What do you think of the idea?

(Some students will likely be squeamish at the thought of eating squirrels. Try to establish that such practices may be necessary when there are no other sources of meat and that we are fortunate to live in a time and place where food is plentiful.)

What other game was eaten by the settlers?
What game is eaten today?
Why is some game considered a delicacy?

Conduct a survey among students to determine the game they have tried.

53

Game was an important food source for the early settlers. Of the game used by the settlers (deer, moose, elk, bear, buffalo, beaver, raccoon, squirrel, skunk, duck, geese, pheasant, quail, partridge, grouse, wild turkey, passenger pigeons), which is still found in your area? Research each and complete a chart as follows:

Game
Plentiful
Scarce
Not found
Still found in other areas

SPOILED ROTTEN

Explore the various ways the settlers used to preserve food (**Food for the Settler,** pp. 64-67). Organize the information on a chart, using the headings below.

Methods	Food Items
drying	meat
pickling	vegetables
smoking	fruit
potting	dry staples

Discuss:

How would using these methods affect the settler's diet?
What methods are still used today?
How have preserving methods changed?
What one development has most improved our methods of preserving foods?

Try making pemmican (**Food for the Settler,** p. 64), or drying berries.

Try preserving some berries as the early settlers did. Here is a method from **Food for the Settler,** p. 21.

"The settlers preserved much of their fruit. First they boiled it with a little sugar until it was thick. Then they spread the fruit on sheets of paper to dry in the sun. The papers were rolled up and hung in a dry place. If a settler wanted to make blueberry pie in the middle of winter, all she had to do was take some dried blueberries from the paper rolls and boil them in water with sugar. The blueberries looked and tasted almost as good as the fresh ones did.

"If it is not practical to spread the fruit in the sun, use an oven on **very low** heat instead. (This will take about 5-6 hours.)

When finished, reconstitute the berries by boiling them in water with a little sugar."

54

THE SPICES OF LIFE

Survey the recipes found in **Food for the Settler.** Which herbs are often called for? Try growing some herbs on your classroom windowsill.

Collect samples of various spices, herbs, and flavorings. Include salt and pepper. Which are used more commonly? Survey students and construct a bar graph to record the information.

Explain that popular items such as salt, pepper, and cinnamon were used sparingly by the early settlers. Speculate as to the reasons. (Such items were very expensive because they were nearly all imported. Salt was needed for preserving and could seldom be spared for use as flavoring.)

What difference would this scarcity of spices make to the food?
Would the minimal use of salt be healthful or unhealthful?
What could the settlers use instead to flavor food? (herbs)

The spices used by the settlers did not come as they do today. They had to be ground using mills, graters, or mortars and pestles. Try grinding some whole spices the old-fashioned way.

What is one important advantage of grinding your own?

Compare the flavor and aroma of a freshly ground and a pre-ground spice.

Salt has long been an important commodity. Expressions using the word "salt" have crept into our language. What do the following mean?

- salt of the earth
- with a grain of salt
- eat a person's salt
- Attic salt
- worth one's salt
- above or below the salt

HOW SWEET IT IS

Although sugar was expensive, the early settler's diet did include some sweets. Make a list of all the sweeteners used today. This may require a little home research on the part of the students. Compare this list to a list of the sweeteners available to the settlers: some sugar, maple syrup and sugar, some molasses, honey, fruit and juices.

How would the lack of inexpensive sugar affect the settlers' diet?
What items that we eat regularly would be considered special treats for settler children?
What are some of the favorite sweets today that the settlers would not have known about?
Who was better off, the settlers with little sugar or people today with lots of sugar?

Try making taffy and having an old-fashioned taffy-pull, or if an ice-cream maker is available, make some ice-cream the long hard way! See **Food for the Settler,** pp. 78-81.

WORKDAY MEALS

The settlers worked hard in their fields or at their crafts; they needed to eat enough food to supply them with the energy to get their daily work done. Big breakfasts were the order of the day! Read the meal descriptions on pp. 48 and 49, **Food for the Settler.**

Why did the settlers require such large meals?
Why didn't they all gain weight?
Why were there so few sedentary jobs?
What would happen if we were to eat such big meals?
How has work changed since the settler days?

Write a story about the man who had 73 flapjacks for breakfast. This story should lend itself to an interesting illustration.

The art of bread-making: *first, mix the ingredients thoroughly with a spoon.*

"Work" the dough. Then put it into a bowl and cover it. Let the ball of dough rise.

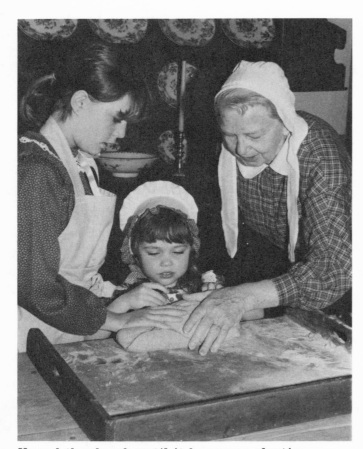

Knead the dough until it becomes elastic; punch it and beat it!

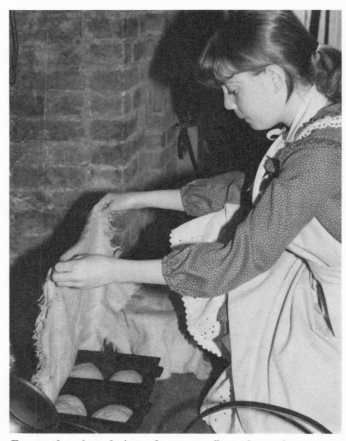

Form the dough into loaves. Put them in warm, greased bread-pans. Let rise again.

OUR DAILY BREAD

Discuss what is meant when we say that bread is a staple food.

What are some other staple foods?
What do we mean when we pray "Give us this day our daily bread"?
Why was the grain crop so important to the settlers?

Explore the meaning of the following expressions:

- to break bread
- the bread line
- cast your bread upon the waters
- take the bread out of one's mouth
- breadbasket of the world
- it's my bread and butter
- know on which side your bread is buttered

WORKING FOR YOUR BREAD AND BUTTER

Making bread the pioneer way is a wonderful way of reaching back into the past. If you do no other cooking or baking, do try bread-making. Don't worry if the results are less than perfect. It's the process that's important.

Use this recipe, reproduced from **Food for the Settler,** p. 38.

If possible, make your experience more authentic by using old wooden mixing bowls and spoons.

What was a dough box?
Why would a special box be built just for letting bread rise? (Rising bread must be kept warm and draught-free.)

Enjoy your fresh bread along with homemade butter and jam.

WHITE BREAD

6 cups (1.5 L)	all-purpose flour
1 T (15 mL)	lard or shortening
1 T (15 mL)	yeast or 1 yeast cake, softened in ¼ cup (60 mL) lukewarm water
2 T (30 mL)	sugar
2 t (10 mL)	salt
1 cup (250 mL)	scalded milk
1 cup (250 mL)	boiled water

Put shortening, sugar, and salt in large bowl, or in top of large double boiler. Add liquids. Cool to lukewarm. Add yeast. Stir in 3 cups (750 mL) flour. Mix thoroughly with spoon. Add 2 cups (500 mL) flour, mix, and add remaining flour gradually, using just enough to prevent sticking to the bowl.

Put the last ½ cup (120 mL) of flour on the mixing board or cloth and use part of the last ½ cup (125 mL) to dust the board very lightly, pushing the rest aside to work into the dough if you need it. Turn the ball of dough onto the board. Cover the dough and let it "rest" for 10 minutes. This will make the dough easier to work with. Knead the dough until it becomes elastic. Cover it with a towel and allow it to double in size in a warm place.

Now for the fun part! Punch the dough, knead it, beat it with your hands for 10 minutes or so. Divide the dough in half. Roll each half into a rectangle. Form dough into loaves. (Warm breadpans by the fire or in stove before greasing.) Place dough seam-side down in greased loaf pans. Brush tops of loaves with butter. Let loaves rise again for about 1½ hours, or until doubled in size.

Preheat oven to 425° F (approximately 220° C). Do not let the sides of the pans touch each other or the sides of the oven. Bake 30-35 minutes or until the bread is brown. Reduce heat to 350° F (approximately 180° C) after 10 minutes. Brush bread again with butter. Knock loaves out of pans and cool on wire racks.

BUTTER

Making butter is relatively easy. See **Food for the Settler**, pp. 44-45.

If you have access to a churn, making butter in the churn would best re-create the original methods. If not, make your butter in an ordinary glass jar as follows:

Warm about 1 cup (250 mL) of whipping cream to room temperature and put in a glass jar with a lid. Add a few very well washed marbles to the jar (not absolutely necessary). Shake the jar continuously, taking turns, until butter forms. Pour off the buttermilk that remains. You might then like to mix in a small quantity of salt with the butter. If you have an old butter mold, cool the butter and pat into the mold.

While the cream is being churned, have class members chant this old exhortation to the butter in time with the churning:

> *Come, butter, come,*
> *Come, butter, come,*
> *Nellie's standing by the gate,*
> *Waiting for her butter cake,*
> *Come, butter, come.*

Think of ways to change the chant. Devise some modern versions and churn to these, too.

THE LONG AND SHORT OF IT

When making butter, keep track of the amount of time it takes for the cream to turn to butter. Then try making butter in a food processor. Use a steel blade and process whipping cream until it turns to butter. Drain off liquid and pat dry with a paper towel. Keep track of time taken.

Which method do you prefer and why?
What other tasks are performed much faster by machines?
Is faster necessarily better?
Support your answers with examples.

Churning butter

MAKING JAM

Make some jam using this recipe from **Food for the Settler,** p. 21.

STRAWBERRY JAM

1 qt. (1 L) strawberries
1¼ cups (approx. 300 mL) sugar

Wash strawberries and remove hulls. Cut into slices. Sprinkle a thin layer of sugar on the bottom of a large, heavy pot. Add a layer of strawberry slices, another layer of sugar, and so on, until you have used up all the fruit and sugar. Make sure the top layer of strawberries is covered with sugar. Let stand 4 to 5 hours.

Wash your jam jars inside and out. Sterilize them by boiling them in a large pot of water for 15-20 minutes. The jars should still be hot when you are ready to fill them. Sterilize the lids as well. Sterilization will kill the bacteria which could spoil your jam. It is your most important step.

Put your fruit and sugar on high heat and boil. Reduce to low heat and cook, stirring often, for 45-60 minutes. Use a candy thermometer to test your jam. When it reaches the temperature of 230° F (110 ° C), it is ready. Ladle the jam into jars and seal them immediately.

NOT SUCH A CORNY IDEA

Corn became a very valuable crop to the settler because it was so versatile.

What do we mean by versatile?
Why would this be such an important feature
to the settlers?
What are some of the ways the settlers used
corn?
What are some of the ways we use corn today?
What other corn or produce would have
been versatile?

Make a "corny" display of samples, pictures, and recipes to illustrate the versatility of corn, both today and in early settler times. Don't forget flour, cereals, corn syrup, corn relish, corn starch, popcorn, corn oils and feed corn.

Have a "corn fest." Cook and sample as many early settler corn recipes as you can. Try Corn Stew or Succotash and Johnny Cake, (**Food for the Settler,** pp. 28-29).

AN APPLE A DAY

Apples were valued by the settlers because they, too, were versatile.

What other crop was valued for its versatility?
What are some of the many ways the settlers
used apples? (See **Food for the Settler,**
pp. 52-55.)

There are many interesting things to do with apples.

If it is autumn, visit an apple orchard to pick your own fresh apples. Bring some back to class and try some of the following activities:

- Have an apple bee! You will need a supply of apples, lots of parers (brought from home by the students — avoid sharp knives if you have younger students), and some help. This would be a good opportunity to invite parents in to lend a hand in the true early settler tradition.

- Divide into groups, each group preparing one of the following:

        apple sauce
        apple butter
        baked apples
        apple snow
        apple crumb cake

    See **Food for the Settler** for most recipes. Have fun sharing what was made!

- There are about 25 species of apples and over seven thousand varieties have been developed by crossing the trees. About 50 of these are commonly grown for their fruit. Make a collection of as many apple varieties as you can find. Conduct taste tests and compare for taste, texture, size, color, and juiciness.

- Read the story of Johnny Appleseed (usually found in collections of American folk tales and legends). Johnny Appleseed was actually John Chapman, who in the early nineteenth century carried apple seeds through much of the eastern United States and helped the settlers establish nurseries and orchards.

A COOKING CATASTROPHE

Cooking today is a far less arduous task than in early settler days. Read "A Cooking Catastrophe" in **Food for the Settler,** p. 57. Have students write their own versions of a cooking catastrophe, modern or early settler style.

WE'RE REALLY COOKING NOW

The range of implements used for cooking has increased tremendously since the days when meals were prepared in a single pot hung in the fireplace. Explore how cooking implements and methods have changed (**Food for the Settler,** pp. 56-61).

Have students prepare a growth chart to illustrate this progression. They might use a combination of hand-drawn pictures and pictures clipped from catalogues and magazines.

GADGETS GALORE

Examine the various items and gadgets used in the settler kitchen (**Food for the Settler,** pp. 62-63). If possible, make a collection of such gadgets.

Have students "design" a gadget for use in a kitchen. Try using such "found materials" as wood scraps, bottle tops, buttons, paper rolls, or spool.

THEN AND NOW

Devise experiments to compare the efficiency of an early settler gadget or implement to its modern counterpart. What you compare will depend on what you have available to you. Possibilities include an antique coffee grinder and an electric one, a vegetable slicer and a food processor, or a lemon squeezer and a juice extractor. Have students write about and illustrate the experiments.

TIME TRAVELERS

Dramatize one or both of the following scenarios. Have students develop their own characters, dialogue, and plot variations.

The evening meal is being prepared in an early settler kitchen. A member of the family is grinding coffee. Suddenly, a time traveler appears in the kitchen. He offers the family the use of an electric coffee grinder. The family must be convinced to try it, and is amazed by the results.

The evening meal is being prepared in a modern kitchen. Suddenly a family of time travelers from 1850 appears. They are invited to stay for dinner. They cannot believe what they see and hear.

SPECIAL OCCASIONS

Discuss the notion that certain foods are traditionally associated with special occasions and festivals. Have students choose three special occasions in their family which are marked by, among other things, the preparation of special foods. List the menus and special foods that would be associated with each occasion. (Possibilities include Thanksgiving, Christmas, Hannukah, or Easter.) Compare students' lists.

Why are some foods common to many families?
What do we call things we do in a special way or at a special time (such as eating turkey at Thanksgiving) that we have been doing for a long time?
What are some other traditions in your family?
Where do traditions come from?
Where might some of our food traditions have come from?

Examine the early settler menus for Thanksgiving and Christmas (**Food for the Settler**, pp. 84-91).

What food traditions probably came to us from the early settlers?

FOOD ACROSS THE MILES

Recall that people from many countries settled in North America (Chapter 1).

Besides the things they needed, what else did these settlers bring with them?

Emphasize language, religion, music, customs and traditions, and favorite recipes.

Which of these have survived to some extent?
Why?
Why would some of these have changed?

Examine the recipes on pp. 82-83 of **Food for the Settler**. Locate on a world map the original countries of these recipes.

What foods and recipes popular today come from other countries?

Make collages titled "Foods from Round the World." Include pictures, recipes, and samples of non-perishables, for example, plastic-wrap enclosed rice. Try one of the recipes on pp. 82-83.

MIND YOUR MANNERS!

Divide the students into two groups. Set one group the task of composing a list of rules for behavior at the table. Read the other group the accounts of table behavior "early settler style" from p. 74 of **Food for the Settler.**

Have this group compose a similar list from the information given. Compare the two lists.

How have table manners changed?
Why might they have changed?
Why were the rules so hard on children?

TRY OUR COCOA

Examine the early food advertisements depicted on p. 71 of **Food for the Settler.**

What messages are the ads trying to get across?
Which products are familiar today?

Look for some current Cadbury's, Fry's, or Quaker Oats' ads and compare.

How have advertising methods changed?
Have the messages changed?
What advertising methods were not available in those days?

Have students choose one food product and design two newspaper advertisements, one as might have been in a newspaper of 1850, one as it might appear today.

A WORK OF ART

Continue the mural begun in Chapter 1. You might depict the variety of foods used by the settlers, some aspect of food production, or the preparation of food.

Chapter 6: A hard day's work

Objectives

Examining occupations as a way of studying past lifestyles.

The community as seen through the work of its people.

Comparing work and occupations in the early settler times and the present as a way of examining change.

Appreciating the hard work and industry of the early settler.

Early Settler Series references

Early Village Life
Early Artisans
Early Loggers and the Sawmill
Early Travel
Early Stores and Markets

Contents

● various occupations common in early settler times; the nature of the work, skills required and the contributions to the community

● how occupations have changed since early settler times

● community interdependence

● women's work

● loggers and the sawmills, the importance of wood, early sawmills, the life of the logger

Notes to the teacher

This chapter would benefit from a visit to or from one or more craftspeople. Such a visit should be arranged before starting the chapter.

If a visit to an early settler museum is planned at this time, have students observe and list all the items made of wood.

WHEN I GROW UP

Begin this unit by composing a list of what students think they would like to be when they grow up. Preserve the list for later use.

Then have students assume the roles of early settler children and have each state what he/she might like to have been when grown up. List their choices on the chart beside their current choices. (Some of these choices will not be appropriate; list them nevertheless as they can be changed later after students become more familiar with the range of occupations that existed in settler times.)

How many of you have chosen similar occupations?
What are some of the reasons for your choices?
Are there some early settler occupations that we are not sure actually existed?
(You might put a question mark beside these for later confirmation.)

Name	Occupation	Early Settler Occupation
Marilyn	teacher	teacher
Hugh	fireman	carpenter
Louise	dentist	dentist
Tony	artist	storekeeper

TINKER, TAILOR, HARNESSMAKER

This activity will provide you with a large information chart outlining the main occupations to be found in the early settler period. Divide students into groups of four or five, each group having a copy of the following outline to complete. Each group will also need a copy of **Early Village Life** and **Early Artisans.** (**Early Travel, Early Stores and Markets,** and **Early Loggers and the Sawmill** would also be useful along with any additional resource material.)

Have students complete the outline by searching through the various sourcebooks for the information needed. One student may act as a recorder.

Occupation	Work Done	Contribution to Community
cooper	made barrels and buckets from wood	barrels and buckets were needed because everything was stored in them

(Note: If limited copies of the resource material are available, have one group of students do the assignment, later reporting to the rest of the class.)

Reproduce the outline on a large chart or on the chalkboard. Using the contributions of the students, transpose the information to the large chart or board.

AT YOUR SERVICE

Explain that while the majority of settlers earned their living as farmers, there were always some who were not interested in farming, especially as villages grew and more and more people moved into an area. These people generally fell into three categories: **Artisans, Merchants,** or **Professionals.** They offered special services to the farm families in the community.

Discuss the meaning of the words in bold and suggest examples of occupations for each category. Categorize each occupation on your chart by putting an **A** (**Artisan**), **M** (**Merchant**), or **P** (**Professional**) beside each listed occupation.

How would people learn the various occupations?
Which would require an apprenticeship?
Which would require some formal schooling?
What kinds of skills would be required for the various jobs?
What occupations would require strength? Stamina? Patience? A good artistic touch? Language ability?
Which jobs would be the most pleasant and why? Unpleasant?
Which jobs would not be considered appropriate for women?

You may wish to have students individually complete a comprehensive occupations chart as follows for 8-10 occupations of their choice.

EARLY SETTLER OCCUPATIONS CHART

Occupation
Work Done
Contribution to Community
Skills Required
Special Qualities or Knowledge
Availability to Women
Degree of Pleasantness

A VANISHING BREED

Many occupations found in early settler times do not exist today. Examine your list of occupations to determine which are no longer found. Have students speculate about the reasons for this change:

Which occupations no longer exist?
Why not?
Which jobs are now largely done by machine?
What occupations still exist?
How have these changed?
Is there any occupation which is almost the same today as it was in early settler times?
How have occupations for women changed?

TIME FLIES

Discuss the expression "Time does not stand still."

How is this expression relevant to people's occupations?

Create a "Changing Occupations" display. Have half the class draw or paint a figure to represent an early settler occupation. Have the other half of the class compose a picture to illustrate the contemporary equivalent of that occupation. Display the figure and the picture side by side.

AND A CHANGING WORLD

Occupations today are often categorized as follows:

Primary any work that involves the harvesting of raw materials or resources, eg. farming, fishing, lumbering, mining

Secondary any work that involves transforming the raw materials into a product: manufacturing

Service work that does not involve the production of a product

Present the above information to students. Cite examples, both past and present, for each category. In which sector are students' parents working?

Explain that in early settler times, most people were involved in the primary area. Today most workers are in the service area. Have students explore the reasons (essentially technological changes) which have produced this shift.

TOOLS OF THE TRADE

Settler workers depended on and valued the tools and materials that helped them do their jobs. Examine the picture of the cobbler on page 38 of **Early Village Life**. What tools and equipment can be seen? Look for a hammer, nails or pegs, peg cutter, awl, lasts, and a cobbler's bench. What tools can be identified in other pictures of people at work?

Have students try to match the following tools, equipment, and materials to the appropriate occupations. This activity may require a bit of dictionary research.

bellows	flax	grindstone
punch	clamp	anvil
press	tongs	hammer
shuttle	awl	scraper
pliers	vise-bench	trowel
saw	glue-pot	kiln
sand	plane	leather
mold	forge	iron

Today many people are engaged in crafts and work in ways not unlike those found in settler times. If possible, arrange to visit a blacksmith, leather worker, weaver, potter, shoemaker, or other craftsperson. Observe the tools used and the skill of the worker. Can any students bring examples of handmade craft items to school? Alternatively, invite a craftsperson to school to show you his/her tools of the trade.

Discuss:

Why do people today value items produced by hand in the old-fashioned way?

WHAT'S MY LINE

Have each student select one occupation and be prepared to role-play that occupation in an interview format. The other students must identify the occupation in a limited time using yes/no questions only, for example, Do you work outdoors? Do you work with wood?

PRESENT OCCUPATIONS

Have the students choose one occupation which they find particularly interesting and prepare a report on that occupation. The organizational headings for the report could be suggested in **Tinker, Tailor, Harnessmaker,** plus a section on tools and equipment. The reports could be presented orally, in written form, or a combination. Students might produce posters, booklets, charts, or bulletin board displays. Alternatively, have each student produce one page (illustration and text) on a particular occupation, and assemble these to produce a class book on "Early Settler Occupations."

WHICH WAY TO THE COBBLER SHOP?

Have students create a sketch map of an imaginary early settler village. This map's purpose will be to show the location of various occupations: doctor's house, teacher's house, saddle-shop, weaver's, apothecary. Have students create a legend for the map by designing an appropriate symbol for each occupation.

Alternatively, have students design a sign to be hung at a person's place of business. Incorporate appropriate symbols in the sign and give some indication of the services offered.

COMMUNITY INTERDEPENDENCE

Most jobs and services in the early community were connected in some fashion; the cooper's barrels held the flour for the miller and the ale for the innkeeper. The nails fashioned by the blacksmith might be used by the joiner. Explore the meaning of the word "interdependent." Have students select ten early settler occupations and illustrate in chart form the connections of products and services among these.

WOMEN'S WORK

Today women can enter just about any occupation they choose; in early settler times there was far less scope for women. While some learned crafts and worked in businesses, most found homemaking and looking after the family a full-time occupation. There was seldom help for their tasks and most became skilled at a variety of tasks that made up their daily work.

Examine the following list of occupations. Explain why each was part of a woman's job in the home.

butcher	farmer	apothecary
baker	chopper	candlemaker
spinner	carpenter	teacher
weaver	doctor	toy-maker
seamstress	nurse	miller

Create a "Window on Women's Work" picture. Divide a piece of art paper into frames to represent a window. Put a frame around each window. In each frame have students sketch a picture to show an "occupation" of the homemaker. (Or enlarge and reproduce the frame depicted here.)

The early settlers constantly needed wood. They needed it for their houses, barns, furniture, and a wealth of other items. Have students examine the following list of items, all of which were usually made of wood in early settler times.

What could each item be made from today?
Which items are now made of synthetic materials?
(wagons, wheels, fences, shingles, chairs, washstands, looms, barrels, tubs, bowls, and spoons)

Have students create a montage by dividing a large piece of paper in half, titling one side "Our Synthetic World," and the other "Their World of Wood." Draw and/or cut out pictures of items and products made from wood or synthetics. Paste the pictures on the appropriate side of the paper.

WOOD YOU LOOK AT THAT!

Begin a collection of pieces of wood. Most of us have a few pieces of leftover planks or boards in our garages or basements. Perhaps someone knows a carpenter who would save some wood scraps for you. Lumber yards will often let you go and collect scraps. Include a couple of logs (fireplace logs) in your collection. Compare the planks or boards and the logs.

What process had turned the log into boards?
How do the boards differ in size? Finish?
Which ones are made from different kinds of wood?
Why is it necessary to "dress" the wood?
(turn it into planks)
How might this work have been done in early settler times? Who would have done the work?
(Save the wood pieces for a later activity.)

Examine the pictures of early sawmills, **Early Loggers and the Sawmill,** pp. 18-27. Using the information contained in the text, compose a "recipe" for turning logs into boards or planks ready for use. Pattern your "recipe" on the cooking recipes, eg. Ingredients (materials needed), Method, and Suggestions for Use (eg. the following planks could be used for building barns or homes).

Discuss the finishing of the wood as outlined in **Early Loggers and the Sawmill,** pp. 28-29.

Why would the work of the wheelwright require a great deal of skill?
What do you call it when wood gets wet accidentally and bends out of shape? (warping)

Make a set of wooden blocks. Have each student select one piece of wood from your scrap collection. The task of each student will be to turn that scrap into the smoothest piece of wood possible. You will need an assortment of various grades of sandpaper. Have students keep track of the time spent on finishing their pieces of wood. If possible, bring an electric sander to school and sand several pieces of wood, comparing the time taken to sand using hand power and the modern sander.

If you can obtain some wood stains (again send your students searching through their basements and garages), have the students stain and polish their wood as well.

Make an artistic display of the completed "blocks."
You might donate your blocks to the kindergarten class.

The logger was the hearty, strong soul who went into the bush, cut down the trees, and floated them down rivers to the sawmills. Paul Bunyan was a fictional logger and woodsman made legendary in old tales. Read one or two Paul Bunyan tales to the class.

Examine the life of the loggers as described in **Early Loggers and the Sawmill,** pp. 32-55. Have students assume the role of a logger and create a journal or diary of a logger's life over a period of several months. Four or five entries should provide enough writing for students to describe the logger's life.

The general store was filled to the rooftop with a variety of goods. Hanging items from a mobile was a great way to save space. See the directions for making mobiles, p. 73.

Chapter 7: I'll see you at the store

Objectives

To investigate how stores and markets changed settlers' lives.

To understand the impact of commercial centers on community life.

To discuss and debate the concept of material needs vs. wants.

Contents

- settler life before stores

- differentiating between needs and wants

- the first store (general store)

- the many facets of the general store: business center, social center; appearance; goods sold; running the store

- other stores and services

- trading and bartering

Early Settler Series references

Early Stores and Markets
Early Village Life
Early Family Home

Notes to the teacher

Trading posts and forts are depicted and discussed as early forms of stores in the following books:

The trading post, **Early Stores and Markets,** pp. 10-11.

The fort, **Early Stores and Markets,** p. 5, and **Early Loggers and the Sawmill,** pp. 10, 19.

Two early North American settlements, Jamestown and Ste. Marie Among the Hurons, are depicted in **Early Stores and Markets,** pp. 6-7.

Town stores of the seventeenth and eighteenth centuries are also shown in **Early Stores and Markets,** pp. 6-7.

BEFORE THERE WERE STORES

Have students make as complete a list as possible of everything purchased by their family over the period of the last month. They will need to consult family members for help in preparing the list.

When complete, discuss where they might obtain the items if there were no stores. Possibilities include: making items, borrowing, trading, sharing, and doing without.

Discuss:

Is life easier or harder without stores?
How would you feel about doing without certain items?
What do you think the early settlers did before there were villages and stores?

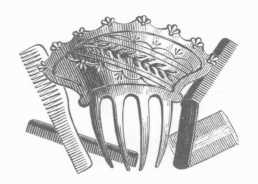

DO YOU REALLY NEED IT?

The Early Family Home, pp. 50-51, discusses the difference between borrowing and trading among the settlers. Luxuries were not to be borrowed.

Have students examine their lists from the previous activity. Differentiate between **necessities** and **luxuries** (the things you want but can do without) or **needs** and **wants.**

What would have been necessities for the early settlers? What would have been luxuries? (Refer to activities in Chapter 1.)

THE GENERAL STORE

Discuss:

If there could be only one store in your community, what kind would it be?
What kind of store was usually the first store in the villages of the early settlers?
(the general store)
What kinds of things might the general store supply that settlers could not make for themselves?
What little luxuries might the store stock?

GOODS TO BARTER

There were two kinds of goods at the general store: goods to be traded for, and goods to be traded with.

Examine the following lists of goods from p. 39 of **Early Stores and Markets.**

Which were traded with?
Which were traded for?
One item appears on both lists. Can you think why?

"Neither a borrower nor a lender be," was a guideline for the settlers, but they cheerfully lent necessities from sugar to shoes. Borrowing luxuries was frowned upon.

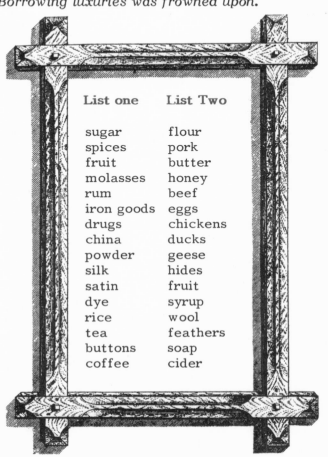

List one	List Two
sugar	flour
spices	pork
fruit	butter
molasses	honey
rum	beef
iron goods	eggs
drugs	chickens
china	ducks
powder	geese
silk	hides
satin	fruit
dye	syrup
rice	wool
tea	feathers
buttons	soap
coffee	cider

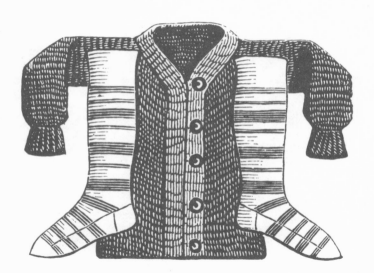

The storekeeper measures bulk flour into small bags. To the right of her is a coffee grinder.

SETTING UP A GENERAL STORE

A very basic store can be set up in a corner of the classroom, using stacked cardboard cartons for shelves. These can be stapled together and fixed to the walls with heavy tape or twine. A more elaborate arrangement can be constructed of real materials if your budget and/or sales activities permit. Parents may donate wood and lend tools. Simple plans for shelves can be found in the public library.

Your store can grow and change as the unit study progresses. Initially, it could contain:

● a bin of goods for trade and exchange with a fair exchange list posted nearby

● a daily news box, containing children's stories

● a postcard center for children to write messages to each other, and for the teacher to deliver reminders and evaluations to the pupils. Mail call can be arranged

● table, chairs, checkerboard games, snacks

As goods begin to arrive (cereal boxes, soup tins, other containers from home), children can make supplies of paper bills and coins for "purchasing" and making "change."

When enough goods are accumulated, they can compose their own arithmetic problems.

The store can be the center for many activities on weighing and measuring, price comparison, fractions, unit pricing, nutrition study, geography, budgeting, and statements of income and expenditure, especially as related to money-raising "bee" activities for the class or charity.

A WORK OF ART

Add a panel to the mural begun in Chapter 1. Depict the interior of the general store, or a collage of goods for sale and trade.

THE HUB OF THE COMMUNITY

The general store was far more than just a place to buy and trade; it became the hub of the community activity and the focal point for a variety of commercial activities.

Divide students into groups. Have each group research one aspect of the role of the general store and make a presentation to the rest of the class. **Early Stores and Markets** will provide the basic information. Include other sources. Encourage students to vary their presentations. Some possibilities include:

● dramatization
● talking to a series of pictures or cartoons which they have prepared
● preparing a handout for the rest of the class
● oral presentation
● preparing a tape with sound effects

Groups could be organized around the following topics. Don't worry if there is some overlap among students' work:

a) **Community Business Center** contact with the rest of the world, post office

b) **Center for Social Activities and Meetings**

c) **Inside the Store** items for sale

d) **The Outside View of the Store**

e) **Running the Store** a family affair

f) **Buying Then and Now**

THE STOREKEEPER

The storekeeper's job involved more than managing the store. **Early Stores and Markets** enumerates and describes the roles of accountant, politician, businessman, lawyer, newsbringer, diplomat, and everyone's friend. The storekeeper can be seen as the forerunner of many forms of local government and civil law.

WHAT WILL YOU GIVE ME FOR ...

Most settlers in the earlier days used the barter system instead of money. Have students predict how this system might have worked.

Why would the settlers use barter instead of money?
What kinds of things would they have for trade?
What would they trade for?
What would they do if items were not of equal value?
Why would the general store be like a bank?

Examine the trade exchanges as outlined on p. 45 of **Early Stores and Markets.** Have the students pair up, one to play the merchant and one to play the customer. Each student will prepare a list of items to trade. Re-enact a barter. Will there be a credit or a debit for the customer?

LET'S MAKE A DEAL

Discuss:

When have you wanted to make a trade with someone?
What have you traded? (comic books, stamps, records, pictures, clothes, lunches)
How did you decide the value of the things you traded?
Have you been satisfied with the trade?
Felt cheated? Been in conflict?

The settlers had to rely on each other, not only for help when needed, but for fair play when bartering.

Read the section, "Customer Relations," (**Early Stores and Markets,** p. 49). Different kinds of cheating are described. In the absence of statutory regulations, honesty, trust, and cooperation were vital. Concepts of fair play, spoiling and preserving relationships, and getting what you pay for may be discussed.

BARTER DAY

Have a barter day in class. Each student brings items (books, games, puzzles) to trade. Allow students to display their wares and to examine all the goods for trade.

Have them set their priorities — the three items for which they most want to trade. Have half the class at a time remain with their goods while the other half rotates around trying to make deals. Establish a set time for this activity.

Evaluation:

What do you think of the barter system?
What problems did you have?
Why did money come into widespread use?

CAVEAT EMPTOR!

As money came into circulation more generally, and as people could move about and buy what they wanted, the concept of self-sufficiency changed. As options and means of securing goods proliferate, decisions become more complex.

Teachers could pursue the issue of wants and needs in the context of advertising and consumer education.

- collect ads for toys, games, cereals, etc., and discuss television and radio commercials

- compare the advertisements with the reality

- encourage the students to question and discriminate

- voice expectations

- discuss ways and means of dealing with disappointment, and of seeking redress

HOW FAR WILL A DOLLAR GO?

This can be a group activity or assigned for individual research. Have children visit a corner store, imagining that they have a dollar to spend. How many combinations of goods can they devise for spending their dollar? Which list gives the best value? How do you decide this?

BEYOND THE GENERAL STORE

As the village grew, more and more stores were established, providing an increasing variety of goods and services for the settlers. Find out about the following kinds of stores from **Early Stores and Markets, Early Village Life,** and other sources.

butcher	printer
bakery	hardware
apothecary	harness
millinery	blacksmith
bootmaker	silversmith
bookbinder	cooper

Who might have been the main customers at each?
Which stores still exist?
Which have disappeared or become rare?
What kind of store would you like to own?

Have students pretend they own one kind of shop and prepare an advertisement for the local newspaper. Examine contemporary ads. What kinds of messages do they convey to make the store attractive?

Is bartering and trading still carried on today? What are some examples of this practice? Remember that people can exchange services as well as goods. Examine newspaper classified ads for examples of people with goods or services to barter.

MOBILE

Make a giant mobile to illustrate the variety of goods found in the general store. Have students draw, color, cut, and mount items on cardboard. Hang by threads from a wire strung across the classroom or from a hoop. Alternatively, hang items in the windows.

FOR SALE

Prepare a "catalog" of items for sale in the general store. Include descriptions, prices, and illustrations. Reproductions of old mail-order catalogs are available, usually inexpensively. If possible, obtain a copy of an old catalog for perusal.

RUMMAGE AND BAKE

The class could organize a rummage and/or bake sale to raise money to finance some of the activities mentioned in the guide.

Organize this event as a "bee." Teams can prepare the announcements and distribute them. Find a suitable location, tables, booths, racks, and boxes to contain the goods.

Decide on a menu of food items to bake and sell. Will you have a refreshment stand as well, perhaps serving punch and cookies?

This event can initiate many math activities, including the principles of basic bookkeeping.

LUXURIES OR NECESSITIES?

Are the following luxuries or necessities?
Discuss.

car
snowshovel
television
calculator
watch
boots
plastic wrap
video games

Do you need another category?
What would you call it?
What would the early settlers have considered these items?

Cut out pictures of various consumer items from newspaper and magazine advertisements. Make groups of individual montages to illustrate necessities and luxuries.

SKILLS EXCHANGE

Many communities and schools hold exchanges of used and outgrown toys and sports equipment, such as bikes, hockey pads, helmets, skates. Can one be started in your area?

Pupils may have skills to exchange with each other, eg. patching a bicycle tire, fluency in another language, chess skills, fancy sewing, sports skills.

They can refer to the self-sufficiency index, Chapter 1, to see what skills are available in the class, or have each student prepare a poster advertising the skill he or she has to offer.

If you wish to pursue this as a class activity, be aware of pupils' inexperience with negotiating, and possible conflict with generous motives.

Emphasize decision-making skills in setting up the exchange:

Is the exchange clear to all parties?
What does each person expect, and when?
Have all feelings been expressed?
Are all parties willing?
Does the exchange seem reasonable?
Is adult permission needed or advisable?

Follow up with evaluation:

Would you recommend this exchange to others?
Did you encounter any problems?
Are you satisfied?

This questionnaire could be distributed as a checklist, or as a guide for a written report, following the particular exchange.

MUSIC TO THE NOSE

"A trip to the general store was exciting to the entire settler family, but a particular delight to the settler children.

Most children had been born on the farms where they lived. The farthest distance they had ever traveled was from the farm to the village. They did not have any experience of the rest of the world. The general store held a magic key that could open up the rest of the world to them ....

They could experience another part of the world by smelling the spices that came from there.

The store was filled with a wonderful blend of aromas. If one stood in the store long enough, one could smell molasses, coffee, cheese, fruit, vinegar, and spices. Together, the aroma was like an orchestra making beautiful music to the nose."
(**Early Stores and Markets**, pp. 34, 51)

74

Enjoying fresh bread at the general store.

FOLLOW YOUR NOSE

Teachers may arrange field trips to a number of aromatic stores: bakeries, delicatessens, spice importers.

Arrange a "scenting table" in the classroom. Place items on the table under a sheet for the pupils to identify by smell while blindfolded. These could include items from the general store study, as well as common items such as fresh pencil shavings or grass cuttings. Keep a box of tissues nearby for any sudden sneezes!

Have children make a "Follow Your Nose" expedition, guided by smells along the route: grass, hot asphalt, exhaust fumes, whatever meets their path. Have them list these, and discuss their findings:

Which smells come from natural sources?
Which come from man-made sources?
Which would the early settlers recognize?
Which would be unfamiliar to them?

IF YOU COULD HEAR WHAT I SMELL

Compose a poem in free verse or Haiku form about the experience.

Extend the concept "music to the nose" by having pupils listen to the blending of themes in music, either as a large group or at a listening center. Any or all of the following are suggested:

The Nutcracker Suite
The Grand Canyon Suite
The 1812 Overture

"See" what you hear!

TIME FLIES

Teach or review cardinal and ordinal numbers using "centuries:"

1701–1800 A.D.	eighteenth century
1801–1900 A.D.	nineteenth century
1901–2000 A.D.	twentieth century

Older children may enjoy the following activity:

HAPPY NEW YEAR!

How old will you be in the year 2000? Write a Happy New Year letter to an old friend whom you haven't seen since you were ten years old. Date it January 1, 2000. Tell about your life since that last meeting many years ago. Enclose a picture of yourself.

Stephen is punished for speaking in class by being kept in at recess. He reads happily as the teacher suffers from the confinement. The one-room school could be quite cramped!

Chapter 8: Reading, 'riting, and 'rithmetic

Objectives

Schools as an example of change in the community to which the pupils can relate.

The school as an integral part of the community.

Fostering appreciation for the quality of education today in comparison with the kind of schooling available many years ago.

Notes to the teacher

This chapter contains a number of language arts activities which can be incorporated into your regular reading programs or used as the basis for an early settler school day in your classroom. The **Early Settler Storybook,** pp. 58-59, also contains five "story starters" for creative writing.

Contents

● the many people from whom we learn

● why schools were established

● a typical day

● school buildings and supplies

● the one-room school

● basic school subjects: reading, writing, spelling, arithmetic

● beyond the three Rs

● the teacher's role

Early Settler Series references

Early Schools
Early Village Life

Early City Life
Early Settler Storybook

TEACHERS ALL

Have students construct and complete a chart as outlined below, each student listing several people they know for each category. Beside each name have them list something they have learned from that person. Examples:

Relatives	*Something Learned*
Mother	*good manners*
Grandpa	*about his youth*
brother Bob	*how to climb trees*
Aunt Jean	*how to make popcorn*

Friends and Neighbors	
Nancy	*how to fix my bike*
Tom	*how to whistle*
Mrs. Barnes	*about the birds at her bird feeder*

People in my Community	
my teacher	*how to do division*
my hockey coach	*how to skate backwards*
lady in the camera store	*how to take the film out of my camera*

Discuss the idea of learning. Try to establish that we all learn and have learned from many different people. Adults continue to learn, too.

Read the students the following story reproduced from **Early Schools**. It concerns a group of early settler villagers who have overcome the hardships of the wilderness and who are about to undergo another kind of struggle, a struggle with a new idea, which will change their lives in many ways. Ask the students to listen while you read the story, to discover what the new idea was and how the people dealt with it.

TO BUILD OR NOT TO BUILD

Everyone in the village, from old Gramps Shawcross down to little Alma Shawcross, had crowded into the general store. Gramps held a special place in the community. He had been the first settler in the area, and the first to become a great-grandfather. His family had given its name to Shaw's Crossing.

The previous Sunday, the minister had announced that he was inviting everyone in the community to a meeting on Monday to discuss the possibility of opening a local schoolhouse. Everybody was eager to attend. Mr. Campbell had piled his supplies against the walls of his store to make room for all the people. They waited impatiently for Doctor Duncan because he would bring along Mr. Whitney, the young man who was offering to teach in the village.

The minister arrived looking as serious as he did on Sundays. He had the doctor in tow, who was followed in turn by a young man. The minister stopped at the store counter. "Neighbors," he said, "let me introduce Mr. Whitney, an enthusiastic young English fellow who'd appreciate the opportunity to open a school in our district. Now you all know our own Doctor Duncan. He's volunteered to say a few words about Mr. Whitney."

The Doctor Gives his Diagnosis

Doctor Duncan stepped forward. He paused, greatly pleased with the hush that suddenly blanketed the room. "I was born into this community," he began, "and am proud to call myself a native of Shaw's Crossing. I know you all, and you all know me. You also know I've said many times that it's time our village supported its own real school. We've had the benefit of lessons given in the church by our good minister, and we've made do with our dame school. In fact," he added hastily after catching the eagle eye of Mrs. Shawcross, "Mrs. Shawcross has done a fine job with our little ones in her dame school. But times are changing, and our little ones keep getting bigger but don't have any higher classes to move on to." The doctor looked out the corner of his eye at Mrs. Shawcross. Her feathers were obviously ruffled. Mrs. Shawcross was the widowed daughter of Gramps. She was a plump, gray-haired woman with spectacles perched on her nose. She was about fifty years old.

The dame school had been run in her home for a quarter of a century, ever since her young husband was killed in a farming accident. She taught the children while she sewed and knitted. They recited while she worked with her hands. Between the small sums that her students' parents paid when they could afford to, and the money she made selling her handiwork, Mrs. Shawcross lived comfortably. She was not at all pleased with these new-fangled ideas about education.

Mrs. Shawcross Defends her Dame School

"Doctor Duncan," she now said, drawing out the syllables in his name, "I too am a long-standing member of this community. I am now teaching my second generation of youngsters. I myself was taught by my mother. She did a fine job, and I, if I may say so myself, do a finer. Now this young man thinks he can replace me."

"Mrs. Shawcross," interrupted the doctor, "my dear Mrs. Shawcross. No one here is disputing your ability to carry on a fine school. As a matter of fact, I'm sure Mr. Whitney would be grateful for your advice and assistance should he establish himself here. We could never do without you, Mrs. Shawcross."

The Argument Heats Up

The dame's feathers were smoothed, but Mr. Gee, the blacksmith, had his own objection. "I need my boy in my shop," he hammered out in one-syllable words, "and all he needs to know is how to hold steady a big horse and drive nails at the same time. He doesn't need your fancy books. He needs to know his numbers so he can keep the shop's business straight."

Mr. Whitney had thought it wiser to let the doctor speak for him, but now he raised his hand to get the attention of the crowd. "Mr. Gee," he said respectfully, "I don't plan to start a fancy school which would be unsuitable for Shaw's Crossing. I'd be happy to teach how to keep books as well as read them, and certainly a little writing wouldn't hurt."

Mr. Gee grumbled a bit, but figured addition and letters might not be so bad.

Lessons Learned from the Land

Ben Moss wasn't going to change his mind that easily. He owned a farm a few kilometers away, and he needed his five sons to help work it. He had come from England to build a homestead eighteen years earlier. He had cleared his land, put up fences, and built a house. He still remembered the first day his plow had turned the soil that had never been farmed before — not since the beginning of time! That moment when his plow bit into the earth was a symbol to Ben of his accomplishment in the new country. Whenever he thought of it he felt proud. He wanted to give his sons the same feeling.

"I'm not so good at saying what I mean," he said, "but I think lessons should be learned from the land, the hard but right way. My sons need to know when to plant and when to sow, as it says in the Bible. They need to judge crops and livestock. I can't have my boys spend all day away from their proper jobs. They'll learn silly old Latin and forget the land."

"Ben," answered the doctor, "all five of your boys can't farm your land when they're married with families. Shaw's Crossing needs fine boys like yours to become teachers and doctors. We need leaders in this village and in this country, not followers. And school," he added gently, "might teach your sons to feel that they can put their ideas about living into words."

"We Can't Afford a School"

Ben wasn't fooled by flattery, but he did know his boys were fine and deserved the best. Before he could speak again, his neighbor, Mrs. Reed, chimed in. "My girls don't need book-learning either. Girls should learn to keep house. They need spinning and cooking lessons. I can teach them what they need to know. They have to keep bread on the table, and they can only do that by making it from scratch! Besides, we can't afford a schoolhouse!" Some of the people muttered in agreement. The minister stopped them. "Mr. Whitney has agreed to teach for the sum of one cent a day per pupil if you all agree to provide firewood," he said. The amount seemed a fair price. At least it silenced some of the mutterers.

Gramps Makes a Speech

Gramps Shawcross had been sitting quietly at the back. Now he stood and raised his cane for quiet.

"I've been listening to you all put in your two-cents worth when all Mr. Whitney asks is one cent and a chance." There were a few chuckles at his little joke. He continued, "I'm an old man. I've seen this village grow from a crossroads until it wouldn't be exaggerating to call it a town. When I first came, a handshake sealed a bargain and there was no need for putting words on paper to make a contract between friends and neighbors.

"I know I'm not ashamed that I can only sign an 'X'. Nobody taught me to read or write. I know I've worked awfully hard all my life. I have my doubts about handing children books when they ought to be handling tools.

"But times are changing, as you say, Doc, and Mr. Whitney here tells me today that most other towns already have schoolhouses. My wife, she could read, and she taught my daughter. She'd have a chart of the letters on the kitchen wall and drill her while she baked and washed. Young Mrs. Shawcross

here, why, she could recite Bible verses enough to make your head spin when she was four years old. And my wife, bless her soul, she brought something kind of special to those times when we did rest from work. She'd read to me many an evening.

From Crossroads to Community

"Between the good work of my daughter and the minister and all you parents and grandparents who take the children in hand, we've made do here," Gramps said. "But it's time to work out something permanent. We're a community now, not a crossroads, and so we ought to share in building a school just like we share our help and supplies.

"My friends and neighbors here don't all seem eager about this school business, but maybe we can make a go of it with Mr. Whitney's help."

Gramps turned to the crowd. A few still looked rebellious, but most were nodding and smiling. Little Alma was sniffling, but only because she was hungry and tired of all these people. He turned to Mr. Whitney, and in the sternest voice but with the biggest smile, he said to the new schoolteacher, "You've got the job, it seems, but see you don't teach too darn much Latin. My part of the bargain is that I'll give you the wood and Shawcross land. That is," he said, "if the rest of you will lend your hearts and hands for the building."

Discuss:

Why does Doctor Duncan think the community needs a school?
Who are some of the people who objected to the idea?
What were some of their objections?
Who finally convinced people to build a school?
How will the school get built?

THE PLAY'S THE THING

Dramatize the community meeting at which the school decision was made. Have students play the parts of Doctor Duncan, Mrs. Whitney, the minister, Mr. Campbell, Mrs. Shawcross, and Alma Shawcross. Other students can be other community members at the meeting. Do not attempt to have students memorize the speeches from the story, but have them become familiar with each character's point of view, and create their own lines.

FACT OR OPINION

Have groups of students select one of the main characters and write down each assertion in that character's argument. Have students discuss whether the assertion is a fact or an opinion. They will likely discover that they need another category. What will they call it?

Ben Moss argues that his boys need to learn "when to plant and when to sow, as it says in the Bible." Refer to Ecclesiastes 3:1-8 for the full text.

COLORFUL PHRASES

Discuss the following:

- the hush blanketed the room
- had the young doctor in tow
- we've made do
- her feathers were ruffled .... the dame's feathers were smoothed
- new-fangled ideas
- a long-standing member
- a symbol of his accomplishment
- put in your two-cents worth
- a handshake sealed a bargain
- enough to make your head spin

SYLLABLES

"I need my boy in my shop," he hammered out in one-syllable words.

The sentence can be an introduction to a reinforcement of syllable and accent activities. The concept of hammering underscores voice and body congruity: rhythmic speech, meter in poetry, street chants, dances, and games.

Selected two-syllable words from the story:

village	assist
announce	hammer
offer	little
support	follow
lesson	afford
bigger	mutter
getting	arrive
ruffled	knitted
carry	

Selected three-syllable words:

everyone	accident
general	handiwork
family	recited
previous	syllable
minister	assistance
inviting	establish
serious	attention
volunteered	certainly
blanketed	addition
supported	easily
benefit	flattery
hastily	permanent
spectacles	

Selected four-syllable words:

community	ability
impatiently	respectfully
appreciate	unsuitable
obviously	kilometer
education	accomplishment
generation	interrupted

Selected five-syllable words:

possibility	exaggerating
enthusiastic	opportunity

ANTONYMS

proud > ashamed
everybody > nobody
leader > follower
old > young

COMPOUND WORDS

everybody	nobody
everyone	grandparent
schoolhouse	because
homestead	forward
livestock	become
firewood	blacksmith
crossroads	into
handshake	today
schoolteacher	something

UNDERSTANDING SENTENCES

Phrases or parts of a sentence can be introduced or practised by playing a "detective game."

Print the phrases on separate cards:

The previous Sunday
the minister
had announced
that he was inviting
everyone in the community
to a meeting
on Monday
to discuss
the possibility of opening
a local schoolhouse.

Have pupils sort the cards and arrange the phrases, in order, to make a sentence, by asking themselves whether the phrases answer the questions **Who? What? Where? When? Why? How?**

Two additional clues to the puzzle are the phrases that begin with a capital letter, and end with a punctuation mark.

For this long example, there will be more than one card in some categories of clues. Pupils can have fun arranging the cards to make sense. Can any be left out?

A LONG SCHOOL DAY

Pages 16-17 of **Early Schools** provide an overview of a typical day in an early school. Take your students through an abbreviated version of the school day, playing the strict school marm or master. Divide the students into "grades." Begin with regimented opening exercises and include recitations and oral arithmetic drills.

Once you have completed further activities on early schools, consider re-creating a whole school day, early settler style.

An Early Settler Day at School

Have students come to school in costume: long skirts, bonnets, and aprons for the girls, knickers (knee socks over regular trousers), shirts, suspenders, and caps for the boys. Teacher should dress up, too!

- Plan lessons based on the types of lessons taught.

- Make slates for use that day, or consider using straight pens and ink.

- Have students bring lunch in a box.

- Rearrange classroom furniture to resemble an early schoolhouse.

- Choose a date, eg. September 23, 1852, and write it on the board.

- Play such recess games as "Fox and the Goose" (if winter), "Ante Ante Over the Shanty," and "Snap-the-Whip" as described on p. 30 of **Early Schools.**

- Play the games "Buzz Buzz" and "Clap or Hiss" as described on p. 23 of **Early Schools.**

- There were no desks; students sat on rough pine benches with no backs.
- Parents provided firewood for the stove; sometimes they forgot!
- There were no school buses; students walked long distances.

Have students write present-day correlatives for the above statements. Would they rather go to school now or in the days of the settlers?

WHEN YOU WROTE ON MY SLATE

School supplies were simple and scarce. See pp. 14-15 of **Early Schools.** Have students try to make and use some of the early materials.

Slates Cut a piece of heavy cardboard (corrugated) or plywood. Paint with flat black paint. Make a "frame" of masking tape or narrow strips of wood.

Notebooks Make notebooks as outlined on p. 14 of **Early Schools.**

Quill Pen If a large feather is available, sharpen the end and try to write with it. You'll need some ink, and a little perseverence!

Often someone in the community will have a copy or a reproduction of an old reader. Try to obtain one and examine it.

ONE ROOM, EIGHT GRADES

The one-room schoolhouse: one teacher, all grades, and students ranging in age from five to fifteen and older.

What would be some of the advantages of being all together?
What are some of the problems in this system?
Would you like to go to school this way? Why/Why not?

One of the advantages of the one-room school was that older students were available to help younger students with their reading or with sums. Arrange to have your students spend some time helping out in a younger class. Later, have students analyze their experience. Who learned the most?

SET THE STAGE

Children could write a play, based on early settler school days, and present it to a special audience simply for enjoyment, or as part of a fund-raising bee.

Arrange to have several students "misbehave" in the play, and re-enact some typical punishments, including a "dunce" cap, a simulated "caning," or sending a note home.

Invite visitors, other students, parents, your principal, the librarian, to observe your activities.

THE FIRST SCHOOLHOUSES

Present students with the following list of statements describing aspects of the early schoolhouse. Discuss the possible reasons for, and implications of these conditions. Refer to **Early Schools,** pp. 10-13.

- Schools were built on land that was not suitable for farming.
- Schoolhouses were made of logs; wind whistled through the building.
- Sometimes it was so cold that the ink froze in the inkwells.
- The early schoolhouses were heated by smoky fires or stoves.

MIXED AGES

Re-create the one-room school situation. Arrange with a teacher of younger or older students to share classes for a morning or afternoon. Mix the students, each teacher being responsible for one mixed class. Better still, involve several teachers of varied age groups, creating a real mix of students.

DO YOU KNOW YOUR ABCs?

Distribute the alphabet rhyme, reproduced from p. 19 of **Early Schools.** Have students read chorally, each group taking one verse in turn. Notice that there is no rhyme for words spelled with "x".

From A to Z

A is in always, but not in ever;
  It is in part, but not in sever.

B is in bind, but not in tie;
  It is in bawl, but not in cry.

C is in certain, but not in sure;
  It is in clean, but not in pure.

D is in din, but not in noise;
  It is in lads, but not in boys.

E is in evil, but not in bad;
  It is in grieved, but not in sad.

F is in fountain, but not in spring;
  It is in fetch, but not in bring.

G is in gladness, but not in joy;
  It is in plaything, but not in toy.

H is in hue, but not in tinge;
  It is in scorch, but not in singe.

I is in incense, but not in enrage;
  It is in wise, but not in sage.

J is in juicy, but not in sappy;
  It is in joyous, but not in happy.

K is in keep, but not in retain;
  It is in killed, but not in slain.

L is in lance, but not in spear;
  It is in lake, but not in mere.

M is in meet, but not in fit;
  It is in wisdom, but not in wit.

N is in naughty, but not in bad;
  It is in maniac, but not in mad.

O is in odor, but not in scent;
  It is in bowed, but not in bent.

P is in prophet, but not in seer;
  It is in precious, but not in dear.

Q is in quiver, but not in shake;
  It is in quench, but not in slake.

R is in rapine, but not in pillage;
  It is in culture, but not in tillage.

S is in sewer, but not in drain;
  It is in suffering, but not in pain.

T is in twelve, but not in dozen;
  It is in cheat, but not in cozen.

U is in utter, but not in speak;
  It is in summit, but not in peak.

V is in view, but not in scene;
  It is in verdant, but not in green.

W is in wed, but not in marry;
  It is in wait, but not in tarry.

Y is in yawn, but not in gape;
  It is in monkey, but not in ape.

Z is in zebra, but not in horse;
  It is in furze, but not in gorse.

READING AND WRITING

Penmanship was a prized skill: students spent hours perfecting their handwriting. See p. 20, **Early Schools.** Have students write a special compositon in their best handwriting, decorating the borders with designs, as done by students long ago. Display the students' efforts.

Explain that in later years, pupils wrote with straight pens with nibs and ink. Obtain some pens, nibs, and ink. Try an art-supply store. Have students try writing with these materials. Who can make the fewest blots?

Use a saying or expression with a moral as text for the writing, eg. "Procrastination is the thief of time."

Read the third reader excerpt on p. 21 of **Early Schools.** What lesson is this brief passage trying to teach?

Examine the rebus on p. 23 of **Early Schools.** Have students select a favorite passage or part of a story and write it in rebus form.

Students were asked to memorize a great deal, often memorizing poems for recitations. Have your students select a favorite poem, perhaps one of the poems from **Early Schools** or **Early Settler Storybook**, memorize it, and recite for the class. (Students who are particularly uncomfortable with this task might prefer to "recite" into the tape recorder.)

SPELLBOUND

In the early schools the ability to spell was of great importance. Refer to pp. 25-26 of **Early Schools.**

The spelling match occupied many an afternoon in early schools. Organize a spelling match in your classroom. Afterwards, have students analyze the activity. Is this a good way to learn? Why? Why not?

The following words appeared in a commonly used nineteenth-century speller. Present the list to students.

Discuss:

Which words are still in use today?
What are the meanings of the unfamiliar words?
Why are some of these words rarely used nowadays?

Words about Home

parlor	veranda
pantry	crockery
victuals	counterpane
bolster	washstand
threshold	skillet
cruet	tinware
kindling	flatiron

Words about Clothing

frock	pelisse
sash	bodice
surplice	wrapper
chemise	waistcoat
hose	gaiters
leggings	muff
breeches	drawers

Have students compose a list of words in common use today that, in their opinion, would not have been known to early settler children.

Reproduce for each student a copy of the following sample lesson from a popular fourth reader of the mid-nineteenth century. Conduct a reading lesson using the story. Remember to place a great emphasis on oral reading.

WHERE THERE'S A WILL, THERE'S A WAY

From **Annotated McGuffey**

1 Henry Bond was about ten years old when his father died. His mother found it difficult to provide for the support of a large family, thus left entirely in her care. By good management, however, she contrived to do so, and also to send Henry, the oldest, to school, and to supply him, for the most part, with such books as he needed.

2 At one time, however, Henry wanted a grammar, in order to join a class in that study, and his mother could not furnish him with the money to buy it. He was very much troubled about it, and went to bed with a heavy heart, thinking what could be done.

3 On waking in the morning, he found that a deep snow had fallen, and the cold wind was blowing furiously. "Ah," said he, "it is an ill wind that blows nobody good."

4 He rose, ran to the house of a neighbor, and offered his service to clear a path around his premises. The offer was accepted. Having completed this work, and received his pay, he went to another place for the same purpose, and then to another, until he had earned enough to buy a grammar.

5 When school commenced, Henry was in his seat, the happiest boy there, ready to begin the lesson in his new book.

6 From that time, Henry was always the first in all his classes. He knew no such word as fail, but always succeeded in all he attempted. Having the will, he always found the way.

Note This fourth reader sold for 75 cents at a time when the average daily wage for a laborer was 50 cents.

Books for learning to read were a scarce and expensive commodity. For many students, especially in the earlier days, the Bible was the only book they ever read. Eventually readers became more widely available.

Discuss:

What lesson does this story try to teach?

What is meant by "an ill wind blows nobody good"?
How many of you would act as Henry did?

Have students devise other stories to teach the moral "Where there is a will, there is a way."

THEY CALLED IT ARITHMETIC

Have students examine pp. 26-27 of **Early Schools,** or present the poem on p. 26. Which terms are familiar or unfamiliar to students? How do they think learning in mathematics is different today?

Early schools often made extensive use of the abacus. If an abacus is available, try some mathematics activities using the abacus.

Try the number tricks and teasers on p. 27 of **Early Schools.**

A WORK OF ART

Have students create another panel for the mural begun in Chapter 1. Depict a scene from an early schoolroom.

RECESS FUN

Discuss the recess games described on pp. 30-31 of **Early Schools.** Try playing some of the games.

Share with the students some of the recess games you remember from your school days.

Have students interview their parents and grandparents about the school-yard games they remember.

How many games are still played today? How have the games changed?

Have students prepare a handbook of "Recess Games and Activities — Then and Now," writing descriptions of the games and illustrating them.

IT'S NOT FAIR

For many years, early school laws required that only boys need attend school. Attendance for girls was optional.

Why do you think this was the case?
Was it fair or unfair? Give reasons.

Have students write about their impressions of those early laws.

IT'S THE LAW

Early school laws varied with respect to compulsory attendance. Research present school laws in your area.

Who must attend school? For how long?
What are the starting and finishing ages?
How long is the official school year?

HOW DOES IT FEEL?

Much emphasis is placed on the uncomfortable conditions in the early schools: hard chairs, no back rests, freezing in winter, stuffy and hot in summer.

Examine the pictures of children's faces in the early settler sketches and photos of school groups.

What else besides miserable physical conditions is making these children so unhappy?
(fear of the schoolmaster's harsh punishments)

Discuss such punishments as having to wear the dunce cap, being beaten in front of the rest of the class, and having to stand in the corner.

What emotions could these cause?
- fear
- embarrassment
- shame
- anger
- helplessness

Would these punishments help the children learn their school work more effectively?
What sorts of fears do you have?

(Children may more willingly discuss their fears than their shames and embarrassments.)

Discuss their ways of dealing with unpleasant situations. Add to the "feelings" chart.

If the class has made a picture collection of gestures and expressions of feeling (Chapter 1), have them examine it. Make up a sentence or two to speculate on what is happening to elicit the feeling being depicted.

Put words for feelings on cards and have students select one to act out or pantomime for the rest of the class. Only actions, gestures, and facial expressions are allowed — no words or sounds.

SCHOOL RULES

Examine the rules for teachers and students, reproduced from pp. 42-43 of **Early Schools.**

How many of these are still good rules?

Have students write a set of rules for teachers or students today. Each half of the class could write one set.

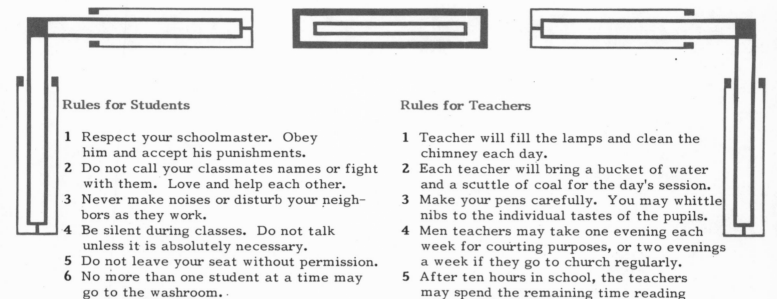

Rules for Students

1 Respect your schoolmaster. Obey him and accept his punishments.
2 Do not call your classmates names or fight with them. Love and help each other.
3 Never make noises or disturb your neighbors as they work.
4 Be silent during classes. Do not talk unless it is absolutely necessary.
5 Do not leave your seat without permission.
6 No more than one student at a time may go to the washroom.
7 At the end of the class, wash your hands and face. Wash your feet if they are bare.
8 Bring firewood into the classroom for the stove whenever the teacher tells you to.
9 Go quietly in and out of the classroom.
10 If the master calls your name after class, straighten out the benches and tables. Sweep the room, dust, and leave everything tidy.

Rules for Teachers

1 Teacher will fill the lamps and clean the chimney each day.
2 Each teacher will bring a bucket of water and a scuttle of coal for the day's session.
3 Make your pens carefully. You may whittle nibs to the individual tastes of the pupils.
4 Men teachers may take one evening each week for courting purposes, or two evenings a week if they go to church regularly.
5 After ten hours in school, the teachers may spend the remaining time reading the Bible or other good books.
6 Women teachers who marry or engage in improper conduct will be dismissed.
7 Every teacher should lay aside from each day's pay a goodly sum of his earnings. He should use his savings during his retirement years so that he will not become a burden on society.
8 Any teacher who smokes, uses liquor in any form, visits pool halls or public halls, or gets shaved in a barber shop, will give good reasons for people to suspect his worth, intentions, and honesty.
9 The teacher who performs his labor faithfully and without fault for five years will be given an increase of 25 cents per week in his pay.

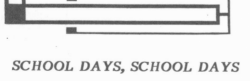

SCHOOL DAYS, SCHOOL DAYS

Learn the song "School Days." What is meant by the following?

● dear old golden rule days
● taught to the tune of the hickory stick
● you were my bashful barefoot beau
● I was your queen in calico

BETTER WAYS TO LEARN

Examine the problems outlined on p. 32 of **Early Schools.** Which problems still exist today?

Have students compose a similar list of "problems" in schools today.

88

BUSY FINGERS

Have students examine the positions of the children's hands in the "school" pictures. (All are visible and folded, or visible and occupied, but definitely visible.)

What unspoken rules are they obeying?
(Don't fidget, don't play, don't make a noise; do what everyone else is doing. Children will have their own interpretations.)

Make a collage of hands. Show them at work, at play, at worship.

Assemble a "Please Touch" table. Include sandpaper, a fuzzy leaf, petroleum jelly, velvet, corduroy, and any other found materials that invite tactile experiences.

Start a list of "touch" words:

    rough
    smooth
    fuzzy
    prickly
    furry
    hairy

HANDY VOCABULARY

Present these figurative uses of "hand" to the class for discussion or for individual research. Find another way of saying:

1 Our class worked hard to put on a play. Every one of us lent a hand. The audience enjoyed it. They gave us a big hand when it was over.

2 Our team practised hard for the big game. We won hands down.

3 Last night a storm damaged the school. We had to stay home today. I have plenty of time on my hands.

4 Joe and Mary did a fine job all by themselves. You really have to hand it to them.

5 Jack never seems to have any money. He lives from hand to mouth.

6 Jane is afraid of Beth. Whenever they are together, Beth has the upper hand.

7 Yesterday we played cards. Sue had the best hand in every game.

8 On a rainy day, an umbrella comes in handy.

Have a helping hands work bee. If seasonally appropriate, clean up the school yard. Be sure that everyone wears gloves for safety.

TEACHING: NOT AN EASY JOB

Read "The Sacrifice of the Schoolmaster" on p. 37 of **Early Schools.**

What information from this story indicates that the work of the teacher was not easy? What other things might make the teacher's life a hard one?

Have a group of students research the teacher's life, using pp. 34-42 of **Early Schools** and any other available information. Have the information presented to the class.

Do you think teachers today have an easy or a difficult lot?
(Be prepared; they probably think you have an easy time of it.)

WHAT ARE YOU WORTH?

Teachers were sometimes paid in food produce in lieu of money. Have your students calculate a month's salary for you if you were paid in food.

Chapter 9: Little adults

Objectives

The lives of children as a way of learning about the past.

Changes in attitudes toward children and child-rearing practices.

Contents

- attitudes and child-rearing practices
- extended families
- discipline and punishment
- babies and young children
- work and chores
- homeless children
- child labor
- play and leisure

Notes to the teacher

A considerable portion of this chapter looks at families and child-rearing practices. Some of the children in your class may come from less than ideal home situations. The teacher will need to be sensitive to any topics or questions that might make some children feel uncomfortable.

This chapter does not deal with schooling, which was explored in the previous chapter. If you did not use that chapter you may wish to include some of the activities from it at this time.

Early Settler Series references

Early Settler Children
Pleasures and Pastimes
Early Settler Storybook
Early Farm Life
Early City Life

UNDER THE SAME ROOF

Early settler families were usually "extended" families, that is parents, children, grandparents, and even aunts and uncles shared the same home. Refer to **Pleasures and Pastimes,** p. 12, and **The Early Family Home,** pp. 34-35. Survey the class to find out how many children live in an extended family situation. Most will probably live with their "nuclear" family, that is, parents and children only.

Why was the typical family structure different in settler times?
Which situation would you prefer? Why?
What would be the advantages and disadvantages of living in a large family?

Discuss:

● how families become larger and smaller
● what activities families share, regardless of size
● how family size affects some activities

What helped large groups of adults and children to live together happily?
(Strict rules of behavior helped everyone know just what roles they were to play within the family.)

On a slip of paper, have each student write one rule for family behavior which is common in their own household. Collect these. Duplicate the suggested rules (eliminating any repetition) and distribute a copy to each student. Divide students into groups and ask them to classify the rules in as many ways as they can. Possibilities include strict, relaxed; rules for children only, rules for everyone.

Discuss:

Which rules would not likely be found in an early settler household? Why not?

GRANDMA AND GRANDPA

In early settler times grandparents usually lived with the family and consequently played an important role, particularly with respect to bringing up the children. Children then saw a great deal more of their grandparents than most children do nowadays. Examine and discuss the pictures on pp. 10-11 of **Early Settler Children.**

Have students plan to interview one of their own grandparents about the childhood of that grandparent. The questions should be well thought out ahead of time. Students who do not have a grandparent living nearby might write a letter to a grandparent asking about his/her childhood. Students who do not have a grandparent might have an older neighbor or other relative who would be happy to be interviewed.

BABY FACTS

Discuss the information about babies presented in the "bubbles" on pp. 12-13 of **Early Settler Children.** What would be the contemporary equivalent of the information presented in each bubble? (This may require a search for further information; perhaps some parents or the school nurse can be of help.)

Make large "bubbles" out of pale blue or white art paper. On each set of "bubbles" write early settler baby facts and contemporary facts. Make a display from your sets of "bubbles."

BABIES THEN AND NOW

Pages 14-19, **Early Settler Children,** illustrate babies' and young children's clothing and other items. Find pictures (magazines, catalogs, etc.) of contemporary baby items and clothing. Create a montage, "Babies Then and Now," by interspersing contemporary pictures with student hand-drawn pictures of items from long ago.

Many of your students are at an age when they will soon be earning money by babysitting. Learn more about baby care. Perhaps there is a mother of a young child who would be prepared to visit your class with her baby and talk about baby care. What modern conveniences make baby care much easier than in days gone by?

91

WORK! WORK! WORK!

Early settler children had far more work to do than most children have today. Your students will probably be quite dismayed to learn what was expected of children in those days.

Working in groups, have students prepare an outline of a week's chores for an early settler boy and girl. This might take the form of a timetable. See pp. 20-27 of **Early Settler Children** for information. Have the outlines printed on a large chart for display. Now, have students compose their own individual outlines of a week's chores and compare these to the early settler outlines.

Who did the most work? Why was this the case?
How would you feel about having so much work to do?
What do you think the children gained from working so much?
What did they have less time for?
Do you think your own work load is fair or unfair? Why?

NO EXCUSES

Page 21 of **Early Settler Children** tells us that children were taught that laziness was the worst sin of all.

Conduct a form of debate on the topic "laziness is the worst sin of all." Divide the students into four groups, two to take the affirmative position, two to take the negative. Have each group write statements to support its position, and choose one student to present the information on the group's behalf. After all groups have made their presentations (alternate between affirmatives and negatives), have students analyze the tasks that were given. Was one side more difficult to defend?

You may wish to try this activity again using the topic "Children today have too much work to do." Can the students suggest further topics for debate?

BOYS' AND GIRLS' WORK

Most chores in early settler days were clearly the responsibility of either boys or girls. Make a list of chores under the headings BOYS' WORK and GIRLS' WORK. Have the boys in your class examine the list of girls' chores to find things they are expected to do today, and vice versa.

Discuss:

Was it better in early settler times or is it better today when boys and girls are usually expected to do the same work?

A DISHWASHING DISASTER

Read the story "Dishwashing — a Disaster," p. 27, **Early Settler Children.** Have students write "disaster" stories for other chores, eg. "A Candlemaking Disaster," "A Bread-Baking Disaster," "A Taming the Horse Disaster." Provide plenty of opportunity for discussion before writing: what were the "disasters" that could occur as settler children went about their work? The cover picture of **Early Settler Storybook** might provide a good starting point for a "disaster" story!

Taming a horse could turn into a disaster! Have your students write a story based on this picture.

LOVE YOUR WORK

Read the poem "Love Your Work," reproduced from p. 20, **Early Settler Children.** What message is the poem trying to convey?

Have students compose their own "work poems." While "Love Your Work" is presented in rhyme, do not have your students attempt this. Ideas will flow more freely and easily if students are encouraged to write free verse.

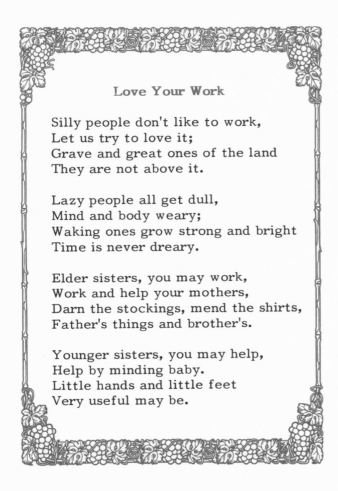

Love Your Work

Silly people don't like to work,
Let us try to love it;
Grave and great ones of the land
They are not above it.

Lazy people all get dull,
Mind and body weary;
Waking ones grow strong and bright
Time is never dreary.

Elder sisters, you may work,
Work and help your mothers,
Darn the stockings, mend the shirts,
Father's things and brother's.

Younger sisters, you may help,
Help by minding baby.
Little hands and little feet
Very useful may be.

RAISING CHILDREN

Discuss with students the following statements which deal with child-rearing in early settler times. Which are applicable today? Which don't seem appropriate anymore? (See **Early Settler Children,** pp. 4-5, and **Early Settler Storybook,** p. 42.)

DIFFERENT WAYS OF SHOWING LOVE

Stress that while children in early settler times were brought up strictly, they were still loved and cared for; parents had a different way of showing their love.

- Loving your children meant raising them to become good human beings.
- Parents thought children had to learn right from wrong at a very early age.
- Life was taken seriously; there was no room for mischief.
- If parents allowed children to misbehave or be lazy, those parents felt they were not good parents.
- Parents expected children to be responsible "little adults" rather than carefree, fun-loving children.
- Parents needed their children to help around the home or farm or go out and earn wages as soon as possible.

BEHAVE! OR ELSE

Attitudes toward children were reflected in the stories and poems of the day. Authors tried to scare children into behaving well by writing stories about the dreadful things that happened to the children who behaved poorly. Read to the students some of the poems and stories from pp. 43-51 of the **Early Settler Storybook.**

In light of the attitudes examined previously,

- compare the behavior of "Sorry Sam," p.47, and "Bully Billy." Is it possible to change "badness" to "goodness" in one gesture?

- prepare a choral reading of "Sulky Sally" or "Bedtime." Have students take turns portraying Sally as the rest read, or portraying Mamma putting the "rebel" children to bed.

- Write the story of Wicked Willie (reproduced overleaf) in prose form, or "try" Willie in a mock court. You'll need a judge, jurors, witnesses, prosecuting and defending lawyers, and of course poor Wicked Willie as the defendant. Is Willie guilty of being wicked or is he merely naughty?

- Have the pupils try to find an opposite for each action and feeling expressed in the poem. This is challenging, as there are fewer precise words for "good" behavior.

Wicked Willie

Willie was a wicked boy,
Snubbed his poor old mother;
Willie was a dreadful boy,
Quarreled with his brother;
Willie was a spiteful boy,
Often pinched his sister;
Once he gave her such a blow,
Raised a great big blister!

Willie was a sulky boy,
Sadly plagued his cousins;
Often broke folk's window panes,
Throwing stones by dozens.
Often worried little girls,
Bullied smaller boys;
Often broke their biggest dolls,
Jumped upon their toys.

If he smelt a smoking tart,
Willie longed to steal it;
If he saw a pulpy peach,
Willie tried to peel it;
Could he reach a new plum cake,
Greedy Willie picked it;
If he spied a pot of jam,
Dirty Willie licked it.

If he saw a poor old dog,
Wicked Willie whacked it;
If it had a spot of white,
Silly Willie blacked it.
If he saw a sleeping cat,
Horrid Willie kicked it;
If he caught a pretty moth,
Cruel Willie pricked it.

If his pony would not trot,
Angry Willie thrashed it;
If he saw a clinging snail,
Thoughtless Willie smashed it;
If he found a sparrow's nest,
Unkind Willie hid it;
All the mischief ever done,
Folks like Willie did it.

No one liked that horrid boy,
Can you wonder at it?
None who saw his ugly head,
Ever tried to pat it.
No one took him for a ride
Folks too gladly skipped him;
No one gave him bats and balls,
No one ever "tipped" him.

No one taught him how to skate,
Or to play at cricket;
No one helped him if he stuck
In a prickly thicket.
Oh, no! for the boys all said
Willie loved to tease them,
And that if he had the chance,
Willie would not please them.

And they shunned him, every one,
And they would not know him;
And their games and picture books
They would never show him.
And their tops they would not spin,
If they saw him near them;
And they treated him with scorn,
Till he learned to fear them.

They left him to himself,
And he was so lonely;
But of course it was his fault,
Willie's own fault only.
If a boy's a wicked boy,
Shy of him folks fight then;
If it makes him dull and sad,
Why it serves him right then!

Discuss the pictures on pp. 8-9 of **Early Settler Children.** What do the students think of the various methods of discipline?

Divide students into three groups. Give each group a copy of the activity sheet illustrated below. Have each group complete only Section A on misbehavior. When complete, have each group exchange sheets with one other group and complete Section B. Again exchange activity sheets and have each group complete Section C. (The sheets will actually have been rotated.) Pass the completed activity sheets back to each original group. What does each group think of the punishments that have been suggested for the misbehaviors it wrote?

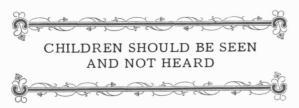

CHILDREN SHOULD BE SEEN AND NOT HEARD

Discuss this old adage. Have children write several paragraphs of agreement or disagreement.

Arrange a half-hour of "business as usual," but in complete silence. All needs must be indicated and dealt with by gesture alone. At the end of the period, discuss how the experience felt and what the class learned. Follow with a rousing sing-song.

Try other activities that are seen but not heard: pantomimes, puppet plays. Read the poem, "My Dolly," from **Early Settler Storybook,** p. 43.

● Run a film silently. Imagine the dialogue. Write the story.
● Plan a visit to an art gallery or museum
● Set up an optics center. Have at least a magnifying glass handy in the classroom.

Then reverse the process. Try activities that are heard but not seen. Tape record part of a TV show, yard noises, school sounds. Have pupils imagine what is going on. Recordings of "sound effects" are excellent tools for identifying activities by sound.

A/ Examples of Misbehavior	B/ How the Early Settlers Might Punish the Misbehavior	C/ How We Would Deal with the Misbehavior
1		
2		
3		
4		
5		

CHILDREN WITHOUT HOMES

The notion of homeless children will be difficult for children today to relate to. Introduce the fact that children without parents were often left to fend for themselves by reading the story "The Courageous Little Sailor," p. 30, **Early Settler Children** and/or "Amanda and Jeremy Search for a Home," p. 16, **Early Settler Storybook.**

Examine the pictures and text, pp. 32-35, **Early Settler Children.**

Why were there so many homeless children?
Why were these children often left to fend for themselves?
What are some of the solutions that were eventually established?
(Indentures, almshouses, adoption)
What was wrong with some of these solutions?
Why are children today so much better off?

Today there are government agencies to look after children who are left without parents or whose homes are unsuitable. You may wish to conduct further research into contemporary ways of providing for such children. Perhaps your school nurse, social worker, or guidance counsellor would be willing to speak to your class.

THE BEST THINGS IN LIFE ARE FREE

Read to the class "The Wildflower Orphan," **Early Settler Storybook,** p. 13.

Discuss:

"The man could not help smiling. Many poor girls were forced to sell flowers for a living, but most managed to find fancy roses."

The statement implies that wildflowers are free and plentiful, hence less interesting and valuable than fancy roses. Is this the case today?

Present the words to the popular song "The Best Things in Life are Free."

● Discuss the implications for today. (Often we have to pay for something the settlers enjoyed freely. Often we mistreat present abundance, not considering that it may be finite.)

● Older children may be stimulated to much lively discussion through examining "protest" songs of past decades.

● Many children have never seen the stars unhampered by city lights. Arrange a visit to a planetarium. Or begin a unit of space study.

CHILD LABOR

Ask students what they think is meant by the term "child labor." Most will be shocked to learn that in the nineteenth century many children were expected, perhaps from the age of nine, to work ten-hour days in factories and mines for very low wages, often doing dirty, unpleasant jobs. Examine the pictures of children at work, pp. 38-39 of **Early Settler Children.**

Why would children have been sent out to work?
What kind of lives would these children have?
What prevents this sort of thing from happening today?

Discuss with students the following statement:

Child labor is a black spot on our history.

Have students draw or paint pictures of children at work, perhaps in mines, factories, or kitchens. Limit the colors used to black and gray. Display pictures with the title "Child Labor -- a Black Spot in History."

POP CORN. A THANKSGIVING PLAY. by Margaret E. Sangster.

The play, "Popcorn — a Thanksgiving Play," presented on pp. 60-62 of **Early Settler Storybook,** tells the story of a young crippled boy who must work selling popcorn to support himself and his poor mother. Taking part in a presentation of this play may help students understand the plight of such children.

The easiest way to do this play, one that will involve the whole class, is readers' theater. For this it will be necessary to reproduce a copy of the play for each student. Groups of students assume the reading parts and, after practicing the reading of their parts, join the rest of the student groups in a choral reading of the play. It will be necessary to have one student be the moderator to read the narrative parts. Students playing individual parts may mime the actions while the rest of the class reads.

Alternatively, students may wish to present this play by creating their own lines once they are familiar with the story.

RAGGED SCHOOLS AND REFORMATORIES

Present students with the following stories of early settler children who committed "crimes." Have them suggest appropriate punishments for these children.

Your students will likely be surprised to learn that in both cases the children would have been sent to adult jails for their "crimes." What would be the results of such a system?

Explore the later alternatives, reformatories and ragged schools, **Early Settler Children,** pp. 36-37. Why were these, too, less than ideal solutions?

1 Sam and Richard Jones were ten and eleven years old. Their father was killed when a cart overturned. Their mother had a hard time feeding and clothing them. There was never enough money for sweets or special treats. One day in the general store, Sam and Richard spied a whole jar of licorice sitting on the counter. They couldn't resist. They grabbed the jar and ran, later stuffing themselves with the wonderful licorice.

2 Lucas Martin, thirteen on his previous birthday, was one of ten children. He felt he never got any attention. One day he was very angry with Mr. Black, a storekeeper who had shooed him out of the general store for being a nuisance. Lucas decided to get even. He waited till Sunday when everyone was in church and the store was closed. Finding a bucket of whitewash in his father's barn, he took the whitewash and painted "Mr. Black is a meanie" all over the store. He also soaped all the windows. Unfortunately, someone came down the street and caught Lucas in the act.

ALL WORK AND NO PLAY MAKE JACK A DULL BOY

Have students discuss this saying. Do they agree? What would have been the settlers' attitudes towards play and fun for children? What kinds of activities were deemed suitable for children?

- *Children should not engage in activities that make them tired.*
- *Children should learn to sing, and play at least one musical instrument.*
- *Playing cards was not a good activity for children: it led to gambling.*
- *Gardening was a good activity because it taught children to rise early, and learn to be orderly.*
- *The best activities for children were walking, riding, visiting, and reading.*
- *Non-fiction books were suitable for children to read because the children could learn something in their spare time.*

What common children's activities would not have been considered proper in early settler times? Have students make a list of all their out-of-school activities, underlining those that would not likely have been found during early settler times, and circling those which probably would not have been considered proper.

Television! What would early settler parents have thought of it? Would they have considered it an appropriate pastime for children? Have students keep track of their leisure time activities for a period of a week to determine how much of their leisure time they spend watching television.

A WORK OF ART

Have students create another panel for the mural begun in Chapter 1. This should depict some aspect of being a child in early settler times.

SIMPLE TOYS, SIMPLE JOYS

Toys were simple, usually homemade or fashioned from scraps. Have an early settler "play day" (morning or afternoon) using very simple toys and games that would have been available to early settler children. The first part of the program will consist of some outdoor activities, the second of some old-fashioned parlor games. Establish four "stations" as outlined below, giving groups of students 10-15 minutes at each station before rotating to the next area. It will be helpful if you can arrange to have some parents or student monitors help at each area. See **Early Settler Children**, pp. 52-53, for further information on the activities.

Stations

1 Cards While children could not play cards, they could play **with** cards. What can students construct or do playing **with** cards?
2 Hoop Rolling Who can roll a hoop the farthest or keep it rolling for the longest time?
3 Skipping Rope Who can "go pepper" for the longest time without tripping? How many skipping rhymes can be found?
4 Cat's Cradle Who can figure out how to make a cat's cradle from a loop of string? What else can be done with a loop of string?

Materials required:
- several decks of playing cards, preferably old ones
- hoops (usually part of physical education equipment) and sticks (pointers would be excellent)
- skipping ropes
- loops of string

Some "parlor games" are suggested on pp. 56-57 of **Early Settler Children**. Play as many as possible. You might also set up a sheet or screen with a light in front and try shadow games.

FUN OUTDOORS

Outdoor activities for early settler children were not that different from those enjoyed by today's children. See **Early Settler Children**, pp. 54-55, and **Early Settler Storybook**, pp. 20-21, **Pleasures and Pastimes, passim.**

Construct two murals — "The Wonders of Winter" and "The Joys of Summer." Illustrate both with early settler children and children of today enjoying the outdoors.

Chapter 10: Making connections --
transportation and communication

Objectives

Understanding the difficulties and dangers faced by the settlers with respect to travel and communication.

Examining changes in transportation and communication over time, and understanding how these changes in technology affected the settler way of life.

Notes to the teacher

Several of the activities in this chapter ask students to compare early transportation and communication to methods used today; this could provide an excellent introduction to a study of contemporary transportation and/or communication.

Early Settler Series references

Early Travel
Early Village Life
Early City Life

Contents

- the importance of water travel
- kinds of boats used
- hazards of water travel
- advent of steampower
- canals
- land travel: Conestoga wagon, pack train, stagecoach
- roads, service to travelers
- the coming of the railroad
- communication: mail service, newspaper, posters, telegraph, telephone

A BETTER WAY

Briefly recall the journey of the settlers to the new land. Consult your chart, "A Better Life", constructed in Chapter 1. From the time they arrived and traveled to their homesteads, and for most of the eighteenth and nineteenth centuries, the settlers used boats as a major means of transportation. Examine a map of North America, preferably one which clearly illustrates the lakes and rivers. Trace possible routes of settlers along waterways.

Why would the early settlements be found along water routes?
Why would the waterways be an important means of travel even after communities were established?
Why was land transport so difficult?
(Refer to Early Travel, p. 12)

BOATS GALORE

Examine this photograph from pp. 12-13 of **Early Travel.** How many kinds of boats can be identified? Use **Early Travel,** pp. 14-19, to find out as much as possible about each of the following kinds of boats. If possible, supplement with other resources:

bateau
canoe
keelboat
ferryboat
houseboat

What were these like? What were they used for?
What were some of the advantages and disadvantages of each particular boat?

100

NOT AN EASY WAY TO GET AROUND

Make models of various early boats. Use heavy cardboard, scraps of wood, and fabric and string. This sketch of a keelboat from p. 17 of **Early Travel** provides a good look at this particular boat.

Boat travel was scarcely a leisurely cruise on a gentle stream; it was fraught with discomfort, hardship, and danger. Have students predict how the following would present problems to settlers traveling by boat.

- traveling upstream against the current
- no wind
- rapids
- ice
- sudden gales
- sandbars
- hidden rocks and logs

Which would be dangerous and which merely inconvenient?

How might some of these be overcome?

Which of these are still problems for boaters today?

Why are some of them no longer problems?

WATT NOW?

Discuss the sources of power for early boats (wind, people, horse).

Why was another source of power needed?
What might that source of power have been? (steampower)
Read the story of James Watt, **Early Travel,** p. 20.

NOISY, DAMP, AND DANGEROUS

Present the following statement:

People in those days were not as accustomed to change as we are today.

Why did it take a while before steamboats became popular?
What sort of things would frighten people?
Why were people not as accustomed to change?
Do you agree or disagree with the above statement? Why/Why not?
What changes or new innovations are some people afraid of today?
Why are they afraid?

Divide students into pairs. Have one play the role of dubious prospective steamship traveler, the other an enterprising steamship captain eager to sell tickets on The Walk-in-the-Water. (See **Early Travel,** p. 20.) Create the conversation that might have taken place. Have several pairs volunteer to present their conversations to the class. Write the dialogue for the conversation between the captain and the traveler.

THE CONTRIBUTIONS OF ...

As individual or group projects, have students research the lives and contributions of James Watt, Robert Fulton, or Alexander Graham Bell.

THE WATER CONNECTION

Locate the Panama and Suez canals on a world map.

Why would these canals have been built?
What bodies of water do they connect?
Are there any canals in your part of the country?
What bodies of water do they connect?

Locate the Erie Canal. Why was this canal built?

THE ERIE CANAL

The Erie Canal was an important American canal, begun in 1817 and completed in 1825. It connected Lake Erie and the Hudson River for a distance of 363 miles. It allowed agricultural goods to move from the east to the newly opened areas further west. Communities sprang up along the route and settlers found the route west much easier. The canal was busy with boats and barges pulled by mules which walked along adjacent tow paths. The drivers of the mules (mule skinners) sang as they drove the mules along.

Discuss the words to this old folk song "Erie Canal." This song is found in many books of folk songs. You may like to learn to sing it.

Erie Canal

I've got a mule her name is Sal,
Fifteen miles on the Erie Canal
She's a good old worker and good old pal,
Fifteen miles on the Erie Canal.

We've hauled some barges in our day
Filled with lumber, coal, and hay,
And we know every inch of the way
From Albany to Buffalo.

Chorus: Low bridge, everybody down
Low bridge, 'cause we're coming to a town;
And you'll always know your neighbor
You'll always know your pal,
If you've ever navigated on the Erie Canal.

We'd better get along, old pal,
Fifteen miles on the Erie Canal,
You can bet your life I'd never part from Sal,
Fifteen miles on the Erie Canal;

Get up there mule, here comes a lock,
We'll make Rome by six o'clock.
One more trip and back we'll go,
Back we'll go to Buffalo.

BLAZING THE TRAIL

Explain that sometimes people needed to travel over land. Before there were roads, people often relied on trails made by the Indians through the forest. It was easy to get lost, so people helped each other by chipping or blazing tree trunks to mark the way.

Organize a trail hunt. You will need another supervising adult to accompany you. Choose a wooded area, eg. a conservation area, woodlot, or large park. Divide the class into two groups, one setting out approximately 5 minutes early to "blaze" the trail using some sort of removable marker, eg. bright ribbons, colored cardboard taped to tree trunks. (We suggest that markers be left at approximately every 50 ft. or 15m.) The other group will attempt to follow the trail, picking up the markers as they go. Arrange a time and place to meet later, just in case your trail blazers and followers are less than expert.

THAT MAN TOOK MY HORSE

In the early settler days horse thieves were often hanged. Why did the settlers consider this such a terrible crime? Was this a fair and reasonable punishment for such a crime? Debate this topic informally among the class.

Read the paragraph "Beasts of Burden," p. 33, **Early Travel.**

What do the students think of this punishment in light of the information in the paragraph?

A LITTLE ROADWORK

Discuss the trails and roads used by the early settlers. (**Early Travel,** pp. 28-30)

Construct a "panorama of road development" as follows:

Use a sand box or salt and flour relief.
Plan the projected route of a road from one community to another.
Construct the road in sections to illustrate the improvements in road construction from settler times to the present:

Section 1 Blazed trail or footpath

2 Corduroy Road — use pieces of dowling or thick twigs embedded in the sand or salt/flour.

3 Plank Road — use popsicle sticks or lumber scraps.

4 Gravel Road — use gravel (aquarium gravel would be suitable).

5 Asphalt — use salt/flour mixture, clay or Plaster of Paris. Paint black.

Build a tollgate somewhere along your road. You may wish later to build models of various conveyances and place these along the road.

Alternatively to building a model, have each student draw a sketch map of an area showing a road in various stages of development.

RULES OF THE ROAD

Present these rules of the road, reproduced from p. 30, **Early Travel.**

Why would these have come into effect?
Which rules are still in use today,
even though they may have changed somewhat?

There were few traffic rules in the days of the early settlers. Below are some of the ones we found.

● Wagons and buggies must use two or more bells on their harnesses.

● Drivers must keep to the right side of the roadway.

● Wagons may not park on town streets for any longer than 24 hours.

● Cattle and sheep must stay off public roads. (However, in some cities pigs were let loose at five o'clock in the morning to eat the garbage off the roads.)

● Driving at unreasonable speeds is not allowed.

● Settlers must mark roads near their property with trees and branches.

● Settlers must clear snowdrifts from their roads in winter.

Have students from half the class choose one rule and construct a poster to advertise it. Use illustrations appropriate to early settler times. Have students from the rest of the class make posters to illustrate present-day rules of the road. Display the posters side by side.

THE CONESTOGA WAGON

Build models of Conestoga wagons and arrange (perhaps along the windowsills) to form a replica of a wagon train of settlers heading west (**Early Travel,** pp. 38-44).

Use small boxes as the base of the wagon. Cardboard tubes sawn in strips make good wheels. Make the top frame of pipe cleaners or pliant wire. Glue paper or cloth over the frame to form the cover. Construct animals and people from clay, plasticene, or paper maché.

Have each student write a brief story of the family in the wagon, predicting what will happen to them. Letter the stories on cards and display alongside each wagon.

GOING TO THE CITY WITH THE PACK TRAIN

Read about the pack trains that carried settlers' produce to the largest markets (**Early Travel,** p. 39).

Play a pack train variation of the old parlor game, "I'm Going on a Trip." Students should be sitting in a circle. The first says "I'm going to the city with the pack train and I'm taking a bushel* of cabbages." The second

*Explain that a bushel was a measurement used in early settler times.

says "I'm going to the city with the pack train and I'm taking a bushel of cabbages and a barrel of maple syrup." The pattern is repeated, each student in turn adding one more item that might have been taken to the market to sell. The game proceeds until one student cannot remember the sequence, or makes an error.

You might play a return version of the game, eg. "I'm coming from the city with the pack train and I'm bringing back ... "

TRAVELING THROUGH SNOW

Examine the picture **Early Travel**, p. 46, depicting the great variety of sleighs used for winter transportation. We are told that winter was the best time for travel. Why is the reverse true today?

Read the story of Miss Muffin's date with Captain Buzbie (**Early Travel**, pp. 48-49). Have students in pairs re-enact the outing, providing Miss Muffin's and Captain Buzbie's conversation.

Compare this outing to the one described in the Christmas song Jingle Bells, written in 1857.

JINGLE BELLS

1 *Dashing through the snow, in a one-horse open sleigh,*
O'er the fields we go, laughing all the way
Bells on bobtails ring, making spirits bright,
Oh, what fun it is to sing a sleighing song tonight.

Chorus

Jingle bells, jingle bells,
jingle all the way,
Oh what fun it is to ride in a one-horse open sleigh!

2 *A day or two ago, I thought I'd take a ride,*
And soon Miss Fannie Bright was seated
by my side;
The horse was lean and lank, misfortune seemed his lot,
He got into a drifted bank, and we, we got upsot.

Have students make a cartoon sequence for either outing, complete with speech balloons.

MRS. MUFFIN'S AGENT

Make a game about Miss Muffin's travels as suggested in **Early Travel**, p. 25.

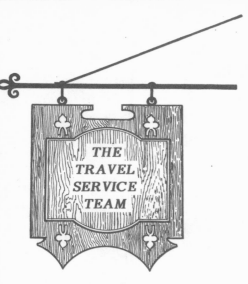

Compare the services available today at most service stations to those offered at inns along the ways traveled by the settlers. (**Early Travel,** pp. 35-37)

Have each student bring to school an advertisement (magazine, newspaper) for a service station. Compare the various ads.

What are they mainly trying to promote?
*What **services** do they focus on?*

Create parallel ads for a wayside inn patterned on the contemporary service-station ads.

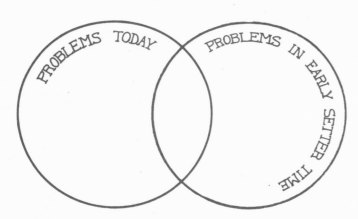

TRAVEL TROUBLES

Draw two overlapping circles. In the left hand section list all the travel troubles that plague travelers today. In the right hand section list the troubles and hazards of early settler travel. (**Early Travel,** pp. 50-55) In the middle list the problems that are common to both eras.

YOUR AXEL BREAKS

Divide students into groups. Have each group design and construct a board game based on a stagecoach journey from one point to another.

Each game should include "penalty cards" based on the hazards and problems of the trip. Students will need to refer to **Early Travel,** pp. 40-41. Rotate the completed games among the groups so that each may try out the other group's games.

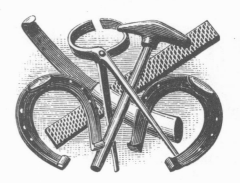

DEAR MR. INNKEEPER

A respite at an early inn or tavern was not exactly luxurious. Read and discuss pp. 56 -57 of **Early Travel.**

Where do you think you would rather stay?
What aspect of these early inns would most upset you?
Why didn't innkeepers improve the conditions?

Compose a letter of complaint to an innkeeper about the conditions at the inn. Do try to find something positive to say besides complaining. Can you suggest ways the innkeeper might change things a bit?

LEAVE THE DRIVING TO US

Use a road map to plot two comparative journeys, one by stagecoach, one by contemporary bus.

Select two communities approximately 200 miles or about 320 km apart. Plot each trip, recording details as follows. Students will need to do some research in order to complete this task.

Compare the journeys with respect to time and convenience.

STAGECOACH 1835			BUS 1984 (5, 6, etc.)	
Departure Point: Time	Milltown 9:00 a.m.		Departure Point: Time	Milltown 9:00 a.m.
First Stop: Time	Pineville		First Stop: Time	Pineville 11:00 a.m.
Second Stop: Time	Logan's Inn		Second Stop: Time	Logan's Inn

Note: Stagecoach schedules of the day show a journey of 2½ miles or 4km per hour.

I'VE BEEN WORKING ON THE RAILROAD

Reproduce the map of Crabtree County illustrated below. Explain that the map was made just after the railway line was built through the country.

What are the main communities in Crabtree County?
Why have they likely grown up in their present locations?
What will happen to these communities now that the railway has been built?
Which communities will likely grow the fastest?
Which community do you predict will become the main community? Why?
Where might new villages spring up?
Which road will become the main road?
Where would you like to own land? Why?

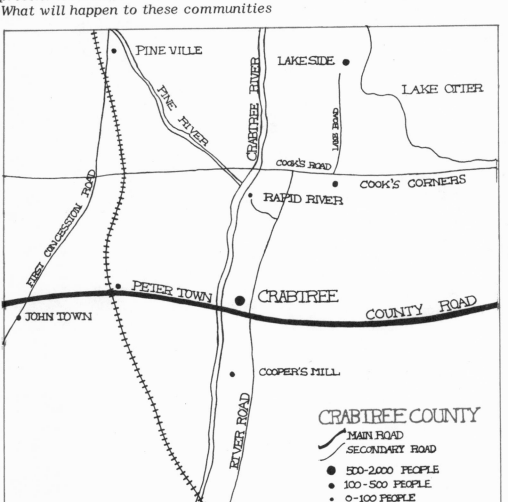

Have students redraw the map of Crabtree County after a period of 25 years has elapsed. Indicate the sizes of the communities and any new communities to become established.

There was no home delivery in the early days. People picked up their mail, and the receiver of a letter paid the postage costs, which varied depending upon the number of pages mailed and the distance the letter was sent. The early post offices were located in the general stores. The mail system was slow, but it was the only way to keep in touch across long distances.

WORD GETS AROUND

As an introduction to early communication, have students list as many modern means of communication as possible. Discuss the variety and speed of our modern communication techniques. Ask students to predict what means of communication would have been available to the early settlers.

What would have been some of the problems with these?

MAIL TIME

Examine the pictures on pp. 16–17 of **Early Stores and Markets.** The following information on early postal service may be of interest to the students.

● The services were run at various times and locations by couriers, private agencies and the government. Because travel was slow, mail delivery was slow.

● There were few post offices. People usually picked up their mail at the general store, often traveling great distances to pick up a letter. Often, news of mail was announced at church or in the local newspaper so that people would know that there was a letter awaiting them.

● Mail was charged according to the number of sheets of paper used. Usually the receiver of the letter paid a cash fee when the letter arrived. In later times when the government became the main mail service, postage stamps came into use.

● Since most communities did not have house numbers or sometimes even named streets, addressing letters was a somewhat haphazard practice, resulting in the following kinds of addresses:

John Blake　　　　　*Mrs. Millie Brown*
Near Otter Lake　　*General Store*
Crabtree County　　*Black Creek*

Envelopes were not used. People crowded as much writing as possible on one side of a page and folded the letter in thirds, sealing the opening with wax and imprinting the wax, perhaps with a personal seal on a ring (signet rings originated from this practice), or with the seal of the store where it was mailed.

Write letters early settler style. Divide students into pairs, each writing to the other from the point of view of early settlers who were friends in the old country, but who have settled in different parts of this country.

Remind students that they must write as small as possible in order to get all their news onto one page, as one page is all they can afford.

Note It was often the practice to write vertically as well as horizontally on a page in order to cram in as much information as possible. This practice was called "cross writing."

Fold the letter, seal with wax, and make an imprint in the wax, perhaps with a ring. (Sealing wax is often available in stationery or novelty shops; candle wax will do instead.)

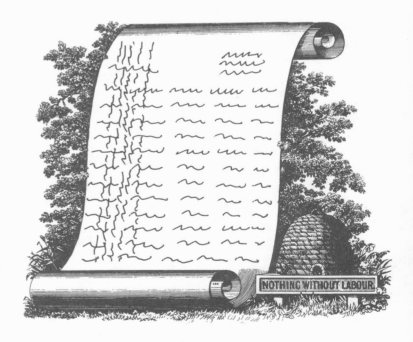

ALL THE
NEWS THAT'S
FIT TO PRINT

While books were often scarce and expensive, many later communities had their own small newspaper, usually no more than 8 pages long and printed weekly (refer to **Early Village Life,** pp. 30-31, and **Early Artisans,** pp. 48-51). Try to find a copy or a reproduction of an early newspaper for perusal.

Research the history of the local newspaper in your community. If possible, arrange a visit to a newspaper to see copies of their early papers.

I SAW IT ON A POSTER

The village printer often produced posters to advertise forthcoming events. Examine the poster reproduced in **Early Village Life,** p. 31.

What kind of outing is this?
Who do you expect will go?
Who is sponsoring the outing?
What else do you expect people will do?
What else would be different?
What important information must the poster contain?
Where would be a good place to hang the poster in order to communicate with the greatest number of people?

Design posters to advertise another kind of community outing or event, early settler or contemporary.

ADS GALORE

The following are some advertisements that might have appeared in the "Willow County Mirror," July, 1865. Have students decide who would likely respond to each advertisement. Are there terms with which the students are unfamiliar?

110

DOT, DOT, DASH, DASH

The telegraph was developed during the first half of the nineteenth century. Samuel Morse is often credited erroneously with this invention; he did introduce relays which amplified the signal enroute, increasing the range of the telegraph, and he was instrumental in introducing this technology to North America. His code for transmitting messages was universally welcomed.

Have students use the Morse code and attempt to tap out simple messages to each other. Record the times taken to transmit a simple message.

Discuss the necessity of keeping messages simple and brief. Try composing some brief messages suitable for telegraph transmission.

The Morse Code

A	—	S	•••
B	—•••	T	—
C	—•—•	U	••—
D	—••	V	•••—
E	•	W	•——
F	••—•	X	—••—
G	——•	Y	—•——
H	••••	Z	——••
I	••	1	•————
J	•———	2	••———
K	—•—	3	•••——
L	•—••	4	••••—
M	——	5	•••••
N	—•	6	—••••
O	———	7	——•••
P	•——•	8	———••
Q	——•—	9	————•
R	•—•	0	—————

Beginning of transmission —•—•—
Error ••••••••
End of transmission •—•—•

"MR. WATSON,
COME HERE —
I WANT YOU"

These were the first words ever transmitted by telephone in March, 1876. By the turn of the century, one in every 50 people had a telephone.

Present students with the following letter which might have taken at least two weeks to travel from Riverview to Lakeside in 1810. Experiment to find out how long it would take to send the information contained in the letter using telegraph and telephone.

THE GREATEST INVENTION

The telephone has long been called "the greatest single invention of the age." Do students agree or disagree? How would life change for people as they had telephones installed in their homes and places of business?

Have each student "create" a new invention to be named after him/her. "Inventions" could be constructed using scrap materials or be designs on paper.

How about the Lang Homework Machine, the Miller Catsup Bottle Cleaner or the Mc-Tavish Mosquito Trap? Let the imaginations run wild!

Lakeside
August 13, 1810

Dear Margaret

I hope this letter finds you and the family well. We were all saddened to hear that little Albert broke his leg. We are praying that it heals well and that Albert will not be lame. He is a fine young boy.

I am sorry to be the bearer of sad news, but you should know that Grandmother has been feeling quite poorly lately. She coughs a great deal and seems to grow weaker with each passing day. I feel it is important that you come and see her soon. She talks of you often and would dearly love to see you.

I know that it is such a busy time, what with the harvest and all the preserving to be done. But you must try to come. Perhaps Mabel could look after the younger ones while you are gone. We could spare young Frank to come with the team and wagon to bring you here.

The rest of us are fine. Samuel works so hard, but the weather has been fair and we expect a good harvest. This year we shall see the first corn crop from the land we cleared last year. The boys are so big now; they are a great help to Samuel in the fields.

I am anxiously awaiting your reply,

Your devoted sister,
Mary.

112

Chapter 11: Box social

Objectives

The simple lifestyle of the early settlers as evidenced by the ways they spent their leisure time.

The importance of the community as the focus for social activities in the early settlers' life.

Understanding that customs and traditions of today have roots in our historical past.

Notes to the teacher

This chapter explores many of the celebrations and social events that were part of the settlers' life. These are much more fun to take part in than to talk about! Do consider organizing at least one such activity — a box social, a mummer's parade, a tea party. With a little pre-organization and perhaps some parental co-operation, it shouldn't be too much work.

Early Settler Series references

Early Family Home
Food for the Settler
Early Settler Children
Early Settler Storybook
Early Pleasures and Pastimes
Early Village Life

Contents

- family-centered simple pleasures

- entertaining; parties

- community events: the bee, box social

- courting and weddings

- word games

- indoor games and activities

- seasonal celebrations; the fair, Thanksgiving, Valentine's Day, Christmas

113

FAMILY FUN

The home was the center of early settler life; pleasures were simple. Discuss the picture of the settler family gathered about the fireplace, **The Early Family Home**, p. 12. In your conversation, try to stress the simplicity of the family's enjoyment together and the notion that they made their own entertainment.

Why would families gather around the
fireplace in the evenings?
What are some things the family is doing?
What other activities might they do?
(reading, sewing, playing games)
Why would it be important for the family
to be together?
Would this family ever use a babysitter?
Why not?
What kinds of things do families today do
together?
In what ways then was the early settlers'
leisure different from ours?

You might also discuss the series of pictures of family life on pp. 34–35 of **The Early Family Home,** and throughout **Early Pleasures and Pastimes.**

Have students construct a folder comparing family leisure in early settler times and today, using simple notes and illustrations. Make a picture of an early settler family in front of the fire. Draw speech balloons and write in the conversation that might have taken place among family members.

THE FAMILY CIRCULAR

Discuss the family circular, p. 14, **Early Pleasures and Pastimes.** Try writing an early settler style family circular by dividing students into groups, each group member representing a family member. The first writer "creates" news of happenings in his/her family and community and records these, passing the circular on to the next person and so on. Later, create pictures to accompany the circulars and make a display of pictures and circulars.

Try keeping a class journal similar to the family journals kept by the settlers. Make a large scrapbook, the number of pages corresponding to the number of students in the class. Have students take turns recording the classroom events and activities for the day. Alternating the recording could be done over a week.

Why would a family journal be a
treasure to keep?

Have students make a journal to take home and have their own family members take turns recording family happenings.

NEVER ON SUNDAY

Religion was important to the settlers; Sunday was a special day of rest and prayer and Bible reading. Bible stories gave the settlers advice in times of trouble, and examples of courage and resourcefulness.

Read several Bible stories to the class. (A "children's" collection of Bible stories will provide simplified versions.) Have students decide what advice and wisdom the settlers would have learned from the stories.

Read the story of Noah's Ark. Why do students think this is the only toy early settler children could play with on Sunday?

Some students might like to build a Noah's Ark and animal models. (See picture on p. 52, **Early Settler Children.**)

OPEN DOORS, OPEN HEARTS

Read the examples of the hospitality and generosity of the settlers towards visitors, pp. 54-55, **The Early Family Home.**

Discuss the information on visiting and social calls presented on p. 54, **The Early Family Home,** and pp. 18-19, **Early Pleasures and Pastimes.** Have students create a set of "hospitality" rules for early settlers: eg. Always offer strangers food and drink.

SURPRISE, SURPRISE!

Settlers often organized surprise parties for friends and neighbors. Several families would prepare the food and drinks, and proceed to the home of the fortunate but unsuspecting recipient. The furniture would be pushed back and there would be dancing and fun. The thoughtful guests always helped with clean-up before departing.

Plan a surprise party, early settler style. Have your class prepare some simple treats. (See chapter 5, **Bread on the Table,** for some ideas for early settler fare.) Dress up pioneer style and perhaps even prepare some musical entertainment. Take your "surprise party" to another classroom in the school. (This should not be a surprise for the teacher, however!) Be sure the visited class knows why you are giving them a party.

Calling cards were small cards with the person's name printed on them. They were left at a home to indicate that a person had called to visit. (See p. 58, **Early Family Home.**)

Why did the use of calling cards originate?
What were the advantages of this custom?
Why has the use of calling cards disappeared?
What is the modern equivalent of the calling card? (business cards or a guest book)
Would it be a good idea to use personal calling cards today? Why/Why not?
What is meant today when we say that someone or something has "left a calling card"?

Collect examples of contemporary business cards. What else appears besides the person's name? Have students design and make a set of their own personal calling cards. Try using them!

BUSY BEES

The bee or work party was an important and popular social occasion for the settlers. The bees were organized so that difficult tasks that would be too much for individuals to do could be completed with the help of a large group of friends and neighbors. The arrangement was a reciprocal one.

Information on the various kinds of bees can be found as follows:
Early Pleasures and Pastimes, pp. 20-21
The Early Family Home, pp. 46-49
Early Village Life, pp. 42-45
Food for the Settler, pp. 50-53

BEE-UTIFUL IDEAS

Have a group of students find out about the various kinds of bees and the activities surrounding these, and make a presentation to the rest of the class.

Make large colorful posters, one for each kind of bee.

Have students be newspaper "reporters" and write up a description of a bee for the social column of the local newspaper.

Who came?
What was accomplished?
Who won the contests?
What was eaten?

PLAN A BEE

Organize a class "bee." Decide on a task that would best be accomplished by a group of people working together. How about cleaning the school yard, cleaning up a local ravine or empty lot, raking leaves, having a car wash for teachers' and parents' cars (donating proceeds to charity?). The best ideas will probably come from the students themselves.

Design some games and contests for after the work part of the bee. Prepare an early settler "feast" as a culmination of your bee. May a good time be had by all!

DANCE UP A STORM

You might like to try some country dancing after your bee, to the tune of your own "music," early settler style. Try to obtain a square dance record to provide the basic fiddle music and "accompaniment" with spoons, a tin kettle, and some tongs to bang in time to the music. Try some paper-covered combs as well.

The settlers' favorite dance was the square dance. Use your physical education classes to learn a few simple dances beforehand.

AND OTHER SOCIAL OCCASIONS

Picnics, tea parties, chicken or oyster suppers, garden parties, and strawberry festivals were also popular. Consider organizing one of these popular events.

THE BOX SOCIAL

The box social was a kind of community dinner which young people in particular enjoyed. It was often used to raise money for a community project. Each young lady would pack a "box" or basket with enough food for two people. The boxes would then be auctioned off to the young gentlemen who would eat dinner with whomever had prepared the box. The identity of each lunch's owner was supposed to be kept secret until after the auction was over.

There was great competition among the ladies to prepare a particularly fine lunch, and those prepared by the best cooks would often go for the highest prices.

Consider having a box social of your own. Perhaps you could reverse things and have the boys make lunches for the girls to bid on. The fairest way, however, is to ask half the class to volunteer to make box lunches.

WON'T YOU BE MINE?

Long before there were commercial Valentine cards, settlers made their own. People who could not think up appropriate messages purchased a "writer" booklet which contained Valentine messages divided into various categories — romantic, humorous, and heartless (remind students that while it might be fun to creat such messages, it would be unkind to actually send them). Perhaps students could create one message or verse for each category.

AND THEN CAME THE CHARIVARI

The customs and vocabulary surrounding courting and marriage in early settler times will likely be unfamiliar to your students. Present them with the following fill-in-the-blanks account of some of these practices. See how many they can figure out!

COURTING COUPLES

Young couples enjoyed _____ pleasures. When a young man went _____ a young lady, he might be entertained in the family _____. Sometimes the young people went for a _____, rode _____, or took a drive in the young man's _____.

Sunday was a special day for _____. A young man would wait by the _____ door to ask a young lady if he might see her home. Sometimes the settlers held sparking _____, where young people got together to meet each other.

Young people seldom were _____ to spend time alone together. A _____ was always present when a couple was together. She even sat in the _____ when a young lady entertained her _____. It is a wonder the young couple ever got around to getting _____.

The wedding was an important event and the _____ often lasted for a week. If there was no _____ _____ for sale in the village store, the young couple might have borrowed one for the occasion. After the wedding, the couple and their neighbors went for a _____ ride around the country. The first person back to the bride's home often got a _____. Later, a dinner and _____ were held until very late in the morning. The young _____ would take home a piece of _____ to put under their _____, hoping to dream of their future _____.

Late at night, when the young couple had gone to sleep, neighborhood boys would make a _____ outside their _____. They played _____ and banged _____ and kettles. This noisy event was called a _____. What a way to begin the marriage!

ANSWERS

wedding cake	bees
parlor	celebrations
simple	husbands
pots	allowed
pillows	fiddles
racket	kitchen
dogcart	dance
married	charivari
window	sparking
courting	ladies
wedding ring	church
prize	walk
beau	horseback
buggy	chaperone

Further information on courting and weddings can be found in **Pleasures and Pastimes**, pp. 32-39, **Early Village Life**, p. 51, and **The Early Family Home**, pp. 26, 57.

Further information on Valentine's Day is found in **Early Pleasures and Pastimes**, pp. 36-37.

Have students create their own fill-in-the-blank stories describing contemporary dating and marriage customs; then exchange stories with a partner to fill in the blanks. Compare early settler and contemporary customs.

118

THE SPORTING LIFE

The settlers enjoyed a variety of sporting activities: hunting, fishing, boating, swimming, riding, and later, biking. The following would be an interesting way to have one group of students make a presentation to the class on sports in early settler times.

Have students assume the roles of sports broadcasters who have taken a time machine back to early settler days. Each must prepare a "sports report" on a particular sport and "broadcast" to the class.

Information on various sporting activities is found in the following:
Early Pleasures and Pastimes, pp. 50-65,
Early Settler Children, p. 55.

I DARE YOU!

Read the selection "Milling Around," pp. 10-11, **Early Pleasures and Pastimes.** Stop at the line "Can you guess what it was?" Have your students try to guess what it was before you read the last lines.

*Why would going to the mill after dark
be a good dare?
How many of you would have taken
the dare?
What are some other things early
settler children might have dared
each other to do?
When can taking a dare be dangerous?*

Have each student write a "dare" on a slip of paper. Gather these and put them in a box. Have students choose one "dare" and write the story of what happened when they accepted the dare.

SHOUTING DOWN MY RAIN BARREL

Outdoor fun was simple; early settler children did not have specially built playground equipment. Discuss the words of the following old children's song. Learn to sing it if you know the tune.

*Come all you children,
Come out and play with me.
Come where the air is free
Climb up my apple tree.*

Shout down my rain barrel,
Slide down my cellar door,**
And we'll be jolly friends
For evermore.*

*A barrel kept outside for catching rainwater.
*Why would it be fun to shout into the
barrel?*

**A sloped door, often covered with a sheet of metal, which enclosed the stairs that led from outside into the cellar.

FLOWER PASTIMES

Early settler children had a lot of fun with simple things that nature provided: a dandelion, a horse chestnut, a blade of grass. Using the information provided on pp. 72-73, **Early Pleasures and Pastimes**, make a list of nature activities and sayings. Are any of these still practiced by children today? How have they changed?

Take a "nature walk" in a local park, ravine, or empty lot. Collect whatever is available and try some of the activities. Perhaps substitutions could be made if some of the flowers are not in season.

JACKS

"Jacks" is easy to play. If a commercial set of jacks is not available, have students make their own sets by collecting pebbles (the way the game was played originally).

A ball is thrown into the air. Before it is caught the player must pick up one "jack." On each successive throw, he/she tries to pick up two "jacks," three "jacks," and so on. The winner is the one who can pick up the most "jacks" before missing the catch.

CATCHING POLLYWOGS

Have students predict what children could have done for fun outdoors. They may not think of such simple activities as swinging on a gate, pumping water from the well, skinny-dipping in the pond or catching pollywogs.

SINK OR SWIM

Most of your students will have taken swimming lessons. What do they think of the instructions for learning to swim outlined on p. 58 of **Early Pleasures and Pastimes**?

*Why would this method of learning to
swim be more difficult?
Would it help people overcome fear
of the water? Why/Why not?
Do you think methods of teaching swimming today are better? Why/Why not?
Why do you think teaching methods
have changed?*

Write a story titled "The Day I Learned to Swim," as it might have been told by an early settler child learning to swim.

DON'T LOSE YOUR MARBLES

Young people could have fun outdoors with a variety of simple equipment such as marbles, tops, hoops, ropes, and jacks. The best way to have your students appreciate the good fun enjoyed by the settlers is to try some of the games and activities using this equipment. You will need a collection of marbles, (these are still sold commercially), tops, (harder to find, try a toy store), ropes, and hoops (usually part of a school's physical education equipment).

Try some of the games and activities outlined in **Early Pleasures and Pastimes**, pp. 66-71. If you can secure enough equipment, why not have a tournament? Activities could be organized round-robin style with "matches" posted on a large chart and students arranging to play their matches at recess and after school.

COME INTO MY PARLOR

After supper the early settlers might have gathered in the parlor for indoor games and activities which became known as parlor games. Several games are described in **Early Pleasures and Pastimes**, pp. 74-81, and **Early Settler Children**, pp. 56-57. Some, such as "Buzz," "I Spy," and "Blindman's Bluff" will probably be familiar to your students. Others, such as "Barnyard," and "Earth, Air and Water" will be new.

Learn to play as many of the parlor games as possible. You might have groups of two or three students take the responsibility of learning one game and then teaching it to the class. Once the games are known, have a "parlor games" social, spending part of your afternoon in some good old-fashioned fun. You might invite parents or another class to join you, dividing the participants into groups, making sure to mix those who know the game with those who don't.

After the students are familiar with a number of games they might construct a "Manual of Parlor Games" with instructions on how to play each game. Have them take their completed manuals home and invite their families to join in an evening of parlor games.

MAGIC LANTERNS AND OTHER INDOOR PASTIMES

Great fun was to be had with simple homemade toys and devices, from doll houses and magic buttons to sundials and thaumatropes. Art activities included spatterwork and illuminating books. Try some of the activities outlined on pp. 83-87 of **Early Pleasures and Pastimes**.

Share your fun with someone else. Why not produce a "traveling road show" of early settler indoor activities, taking the things you've produced to other classrooms in your school and making brief presentations. Students could take turns making the presentations. They will gain some valuable experience in speaking before a group. Alternatively, you might set up a display in the school library or your classroom, and invite others to visit.

THE GAME OF THE GOOSE

This old board game came with the settlers from Europe to the New World. A copy of the board is reproduced on pp. 88-89 of **Early Pleasures and Pastimes**. Have your students work in groups to reproduce a copy of the board, perhaps with a little less detail than the original. Instructions on how to play the game are also included. Give it a try!

WORD GAMES

Riddles, puzzles, jokes, counting rhymes, and tongue-twisters! The settlers had as much fun with these as most of us do today. **Early Pleasures and Pastimes,** pp. 90-91, contains a fine collection of them. Try them out with your class. Start with the jokes.

Are there any you don't get?
Are there any words or expressions that
are unfamiliar?
Which jokes are as appropriate today
as they were in early settler times?

The riddles will prove to be a bit more difficult. Post copies of these and let the students mull over them for a few days. They may need help interpreting some of the lines.

Put your favorite puzzles, jokes, and riddles together into a collection book of "Early Settler Word Fun." Each student could be responsible for one page, to be executed in his/her very best penmanship. If each student's final copy is produced on a stencil, then enough copies of the book could be produced for the students to have their own copy.

 ILLUMINATING BOOKS

The books could be made quite special if your students tried to "illuminate" the capital letters of the words at the beginnings of paragraphs with fancy scrollwork. (See **Early Pleasures and Pastimes,** p. 86, and the examples on this page.)

Trivia games are very popular today. Have your students create their own version of an early settler trivia game. They will need to decide on categories and create a bank of questions. The game could be modeled on a popular commercial version, or the students could devise their own form of the game.

122

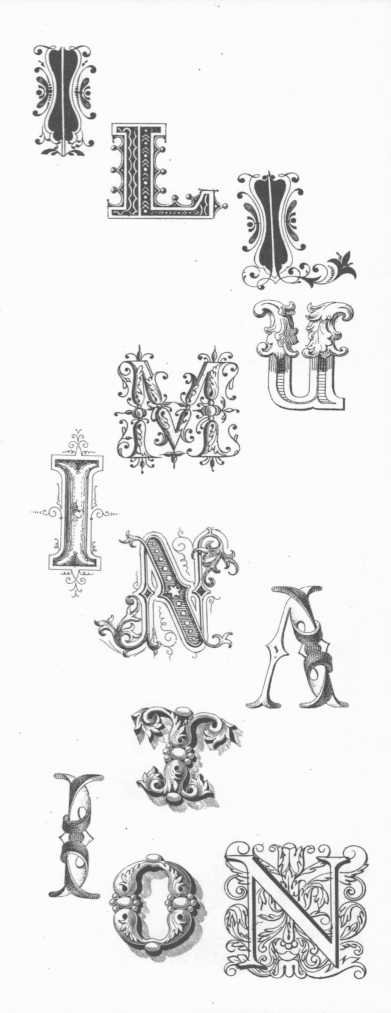

FALL FAIR

The fall was an extremely busy time for the settlers; there were crops to be harvested, wheat to be threshed, corn to be husked, and fruit and vegetables to be preserved. Still, there was time for fun. The fall fair was a wonderful event in the rural community. It included displays and competitions of the best grains, vegetables and flowers, baking competitions, displays of handiwork, animal shows, and above all, the chance to come together and socialize.

The fall fair is still a wonderful event in the rural community, and buses full of school children are usually welcome. Try to find a fall fair near your community and plan a day's outing. This would be particularly valuable for city children, and well worth the trip.

A particularly valuable exercise is to provide the students with a worksheet to take along. Ask them to record the names of various breeds of cattle. Have them search out the winner of the pie contest. This exercise will prevent aimless wandering. Present the students with a few challenges, such as estimating how much the biggest squash at the fair weighs!

Then organize your own fall fair. Even if the samples of fruits and vegetables come from the local supermarket, the idea of a harvest display can be simulated. Why not have each student bring several single vegetables and have competitions for the best "found" potato rather than the best home-grown potato? Award "blue ribbons" made from blue art paper. Include displays of student craftwork or artwork.

THANKSGIVING

Thanksgiving, which was also known as "Harvest Home," took place whenever the work of preparing for winter was finished. Settlers celebrated the harvest and thanked God for their good fortune.

Begin your Thanksgiving activities by having your students make individual lists of everything they are thankful for. Compare your lists and make a composite list for the class. Every item that appears on several lists could go on the class list.

Then examine the list and decide which items the settlers would also be thankful for. Can students suggest items which might appear on the settlers' list but not on their own? Try to stress the importance of the harvest to the settlers for whom, if the harvest was poor, transported food was not available.

Pictures of Thanksgiving activities can be found in **Early Pleasures and Pastimes,** pp. 46-47, **Early Village Life,** pp. 48-49, and **Food for the Settler,** pp. 84-85.

What activities illustrated are
familiar to the students?
Are there any unfamiliar ones?

Many classes celebrate Thanksgiving "dinner." Why not have an early settler Thanksgiving dinner, perhaps in conjunction with your harvest fall fair display?

A typical menu is outlined in **Food for the Settler,** pp. 84-86. Such a dinner would be somewhat ambitious, but a dinner on a smaller scale could be prepared using some help from parents. This would be a good opportunity for your students to wear their "settler costumes."

Put your desks together to form "tables" and decorate for the event with bowls of fruit and vegetables or autumn leaves and cornhusks for centerpieces, Thanksgiving placemats (decorated art paper), and napkins.

Don't forget to begin your dinner with a suitable inter-faith prayer of thanks. Perhaps the prayer could be written by your students.

TRICK OR TREAT

Halloween in some form has been celebrated since medieval times, and is a blending of pre-Christian customs and customs surrounding the Christian festival of Allhallows' Eve. Customs, and the degree to which the day was observed, varied from time to time and from place to place. Discuss the various customs surrounding Halloween described in **Early Pleasures and Pastimes,** pp. 48-49.

Make a display to illustrate these customs by making a number of simple "ghosts" as follows. The ghosts may than be suspended around the room or in the windows, and a brief description of each custom may be pinned to each "ghost."

1 Crumple several pieces of newspaper into a wad to form a "head."
2 Wrap a piece of white cloth or paper toweling over the head and tie loosely under the head to form a "neck."
3 The cloth or paper hangs down in folds to form the "body."
4 Black "eyes" can be put on with paint or crayons.

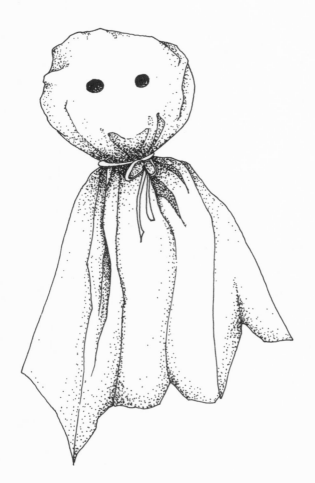

Try some of the Halloween activities suggested in **Early Pleasures and Pastimes.** If it is near Halloween, incorporate them into your own Halloween festivities.

THE WONDERS OF WINTER

Winter fun for the settlers was not all that different from the enjoyment we find today in such activities as skating and sledding, but the equipment was far less sophisticated.

Winter activities are illustrated on p. 54 of **Early Settler Children,** p. 54 of **Early Village Life,** and pp. 22-25 of **Early Settler Storybook.** Examine the pictures and list all the activities or sports. Compare them to today's versions. Have students illustrate the various activities, both early settler and contemporary versions. Mount the pictures on large white circles (snowballs). Glue white cotton batting "snow" around each circle. Make a display of the "Wonders of Winter — Then and Now."

The Early Settler Storybook contains poems which extol the pleasures of winter activities. Read these poems to your students. Are the ideas expressed still relevant today? Try creating your own snow poems!

'TIS THE SEASON TO BE JOLLY

For young people who have come to view Christmas as primarily a time for the exchanging of gifts, learning about Christmas as celebrated by the early settlers may help them appreciate the joy and beauty of the festive season before it became so commercialized. If it is November or December, you may wish to incorporate early settler activities into your regular Christmas season activities. At other times of the year you will likely wish to talk about Christmas more briefly.

The following are only a few of the activities you might include. Information on Christmas celebrations can be found in **Early Christmas, Pleasures and Pastimes, Early Village Life,** pp. 52-53, and **Food for the Settler,** pp. 86-93.

● Read the story of a settler's first Christmas in **Early Christmas,** pp. 10-13. How was Christmas different from the one celebrated by the students?

● Christmas was primarily a religious celebration (**Early Christmas,** pp. 14-15). Make a nativity scene using only scrap materials that would have been available to the settlers.

● Gifts were simply homemade items. Make a pomander ball (**Early Christmas,** p. 18) or corn-husk dolls (see Chapter 4) as simple gifts for students to take home for someone special.

● Learn to sing "Silent Night" using the version known to the settlers (**Early Christmas,** p. 19).

● The holly that the settlers had used at Christmas in their homelands was often not available. Cranberries made a good substitute. Cranberries were threaded like beads into chains and used as decorations. Make some cranberry chains. Try alternating a cranberry and a piece of popcorn for a more colorful chain.

• The children in the picture on p. 20 of **Early Christmas** probably lived in the city where holly might be available. Discuss the picture, remembering how children were disciplined. What might happen to the children when their prank is discovered? Have students assume the role of Susie, Caroline, or Peter and write the story of the prank they played on Uncle Harry. It would also be great fun to dramatize this little episode.

• If boughs of evergreens are available, try decorating your classroom with boughs rather than a Christmas tree, bearing in mind that the tree as a decoration did not come into vogue until the later years.

• Make a kissing bough by suspending a bough of evergreen and hanging a few brightly polished red apples from it. Young men and women were supposed to kiss each other while standing under the bough. Watch the young men in your class avoid being found anywhere near the bough! (There is some question about the historical accuracy of the kissing bough. However, it makes a beautiful decoration and is an interesting alternative to the mistletoe, so we decided to include it in the book.)

• Have a Christmas dinner, early settler style, complete with costumes and decorations. If this is not feasible, make a Christmas pudding (remember to start well before Christmas as suggested on pp. 90-91 of **Food for the Settler**). Can you create a "glorious plum pudding parade" with which to herald your creation when it is brought into the class to be devoured?

• Have a taffy-pulling bee on or near November 25. Refer to **Early Christmas**, p. 29, and **Food for the Settler**, p. 80.

• Compare the lists of "women's preparations" and "men's preparations" for Christmas (**Early Christmas**, pp. 34-35). Who appeared to do the most work? What chores on the lists would now be done by men or women?

• Illustrate the history of Santa Claus by decorating each face of a large empty cardboard carton with pictures of "the changing faces of Santa" (**Early Christmas**, pp. 44-49).

• Learn about how the Christmas tree custom originated and spread (**Early Christmas**, pp. 50-53). Decorate a Christmas tree with simple homemade decorations: fruit, pine cones, candies, and cookies.

• Examine the customs brought by the settlers from their various homelands (**Early Christmas**, pp. 60-62). If possible, talk to people of various backgrounds to find out how they celebrate Christmas now. Have the old customs been preserved?

NEW YEAR'S CUSTOMS

The early settlers actually heard the "ringing in" of the new year if they lived close enough to the church to hear the bells. New Year's was a time for visiting with relatives and close friends. One tradition that the settlers brought from Europe was that of "mumming" (**Early Pleasures and Pastimes,** pp. 28-29).

Create a mummers' parade with your class. Costumes can easily be devised. Remind your students that the main goal of wearing costumes is to be in disguise. Take your parade around the school, visiting classrooms along the way.

The settlers began their parade with a visit to City Hall. Why not begin yours with the principal's office? Encourage students to "keep mum" so as to further hide their identities — what a wonderful way to keep them quiet!

A COMMUNITY ORIENTATION

The community was the hub of a large circle of the settlers' social life. Recall the events that have been discussed throughout this section and list those that were community events (as opposed to individual or private activities).

Why were there so many community events?
Would it have been easy to get to know people if you were new to the community? Why?
How might the community have welcomed new members?

What do you think of the idea of young and old attending the same social functions?
Is this usually the case today?
What events are held in your community that are similar to ones held in settler days?
Why are community events a good idea, now and then?

A WORK OF ART

Complete the mural begun in Chapter 1. There is a lot of scope for this panel. Can the students select an activity that is typical of how the early settlers spent their leisure time?

ENJOY YOUR EARLY SETTLER EXPERIENCE

Enjoy studying the early settlers with your students. Try to have as many hands-on activities as possible. Everyone will learn more and enjoy the experience thoroughly.

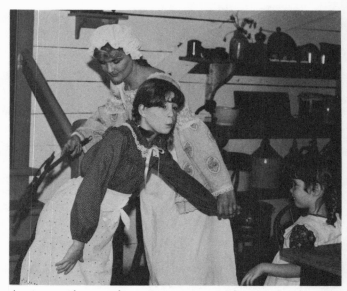

As tempting as it may seem at times, don't get too carried away. This teacher thought she'd try out some good-old-fashioned settler discipline. She enjoyed it more than her student did!

Library of Congress, Dover Archives, Colonial Williamsburg, Century Village, Lang, Upper Canada Village, Black Creek Pioneer Village, Metropolitan Toronto Library, Colborne Lodge, Toronto Historical Board, Gibson House, City of Toronto Archives, Bibliotheque National du Quebec, Harper's Weekly, Canadian Illustrated News, Public Archives of Canada, Notman Photographic Archives, Little Wide Awake, Frank Leslie's Illustrated Magazine, the Osborne Collection of Early Children's Books, Toronto Public Library, the Buffalo and Erie County Public Library Rare Book Department, Jamestown, Chatterbox, McCord Museum, Harper's Round Table Magazine, John P. Robarts Library.

123456789 BP Printed in Canada 09876543